D1529212

Words
THAT
CHANGED
HISTORY

Prohibition
Banning Alcohol

by Adam Woog

**LUCENT
BOOKS ®**

THOMSON
GALE™

San Diego • Detroit • New York • San Francisco • Cleveland
New Haven, Conn. • Waterville, Maine • London • Munich

On Cover: A man destroys barrels of illicit beer
in front of onlookers, during Prohibition.

For Karen, with whom I enjoy an occasional
and perfectly legal drink in the evening

LIBRARY OF CONGRESS CATALOGING-IN-PUBLICATION DATA

Woog, Adam, 1953–
    Prohibition: banning alcohol / by Adam Woog
    p. cm. – (Words that changed history)
    Summary: Profiles the development of conditions that led to Prohibition,
the laws, and the gangsters.
    Includes bibliographical references and index.
    ISBN 1-56006-595-8 (hardback : alk. paper)
    1. Prohibition—United States—History—Juvenile literature. I. Title. II. Series.
HV5089.W75168 2003
363.4'1'0973—dc21
                                                                        2002156784

Printed in the United States of America

Contents

Foreword

"We hold these truths to be self-evident, that all men are created equal, that they are endowed by their Creator with certain unalienable Rights, that among these are Life, Liberty and the pursuit of Happiness." So states one of America's most cherished documents, the Declaration of Independence. These words ripple through time. They represent the thoughts of the Declaration's author, Thomas Jefferson, but at the same time they reflect the attitudes of a nation in which individual rights were trampled by a foreign government. To many of Jefferson's contemporaries, these words characterized a revolutionary philosophy of liberty. Many Americans today still believe the ideas expressed in the Declaration were uniquely American. And while it is true that this document was a product of American ideals and values, its ideas did not spring from an intellectual vacuum. The Enlightenment which had pervaded France and England for years had proffered ideas of individual rights, and Enlightenment scholars drew their notions from historical antecedents tracing back to ancient Greece.

In essence, the Declaration was part of an ongoing historical dialogue concerning the conflict between individual rights and government powers. There is no doubt, however, that it made a palpable impact on its times. For colonists, the Declaration listed their grievances and set out the ideas for which they would stand and fight. These words changed history for Americans. But the Declaration also changed history for other nations; in France, revolutionaries would emulate concepts of self-rule to bring down their own monarchy and draft their own philosophies in a document known as the Declaration of the Rights of Man and of the Citizen. And the historical dialogue continues today in many third world nations.

Lucent Books's Words That Changed History series looks at oral and written documents in light of their historical context and their lasting impact. Some documents, such as the Declaration, spurred people to immediately change society; other documents fostered lasting intellectual debate. For example, Charles Darwin's treatise *On the Origin of Species* did not simply extend the discussion of human origins, it offered a theory of evolution which eventually would cause a schism between some religious and scientific thinkers. The debate still rages as people on both sides reaffirm their intellectual positions, even as new scientific evidence continues to impact the issue.

4

Students researching famous documents, the time periods in which they were prominent, or the issues they raise will find the books in this series both compelling and useful. Readers will see the chain of events that give rise to historical events. They will understand through the examination of specific documents that ideas or philosophies always have their antecedents, and they will learn how these documents carried on the legacy of influence by affecting people in other places or other times. The format for the series emphasizes these points by devoting chapters to the political or intellectual climate of the times, the values and prejudices of the drafters or speakers, the contents of the document and its impact on its contemporaries, and the manner in which perceptions of the document have changed through time.

In addition to their format, the books in Lucent's Words That Changed History series contain features that enhance understanding. Many primary and secondary source quotes give readers insight into the thoughts of the document's contemporaries as well as those who interpret the document's significance in hindsight. Sidebars interspersed throughout the text offer greater examination of relevant personages or significant events to provide readers with a broader historical context. Footnotes allow readers to verify the credibility of source material. Two bibliographies give students the opportunity to expand their research. And an appendix that includes excerpts as well as full text of original documents gives students access to the larger historical picture into which these documents fit.

History is often shaped by words. Oral and written documents concretize the thoughts of a select few, but they often transform the beliefs of an entire era or nation. As Confucius asserted, "Without knowing the force of words, it is impossible to know men." And understanding the power of words reveals a new way of understanding history.

Introduction

The Great Experiment

Americans have always drunk liquor. Many people in colonial times drank alcoholic beverages, especially beer and wine, daily, since the availability and purity of water supplies and other drinkable liquids were uncertain. In later decades, drinking remained a common social activity, in private homes or in saloons.

At the same time, there has always been passionate opposition to alcohol. Many people regarded liquor as an evil that led to illness, financial ruin, and the destruction of family life. They campaigned vigorously to eliminate it.

The conflict between alcohol supporters, called "wets," and their opponents, called "drys," has thus existed throughout American history, reaching its peak early in the twentieth century when, after more than one hundred years of organized effort, the dry movement achieved its greatest victory: a nationwide ban on alcohol. In 1919, a majority of states ratified, or approved, the Eighteenth Amendment to the Constitution, which stated: "After one year from the ratification of this article the manufacture, sale, or transportation of intoxicating liquors within, the importation thereof into, or the exportation thereof from the United States and all territory subject to the jurisdiction thereof for beverage purposes is hereby prohibited."[1]

This ban, called Prohibition, went into effect in 1920; it was accompanied by the Volstead Act, congressional legislation that provided specific rules for enforcing the ban. For the next thirteen years, Prohibition remained in place as a vast, far-reaching test of public policy. President Calvin Coolidge called it "the greatest social experiment of modern times."[2]

The Roaring Twenties

Although Prohibition continued until 1933, it remains most closely associated with the 1920s. This was a colorful period in history, bracketed on both ends by tragedy and misfortune. At the start of the twenties, America was just recovering from the devastation and deprivation of World War I. At the decade's end, the stock market crash of 1929 ushered in the Great Depression and years of hardship.

6

In between, the 1920s was a time of unusual prosperity. The economy seemed to be on an endless climb. Millions flocked to cities to work in booming factories. People had enough money to buy amazing new devices such as radios, refrigerators, and washing machines. Even the poorest family could afford a car, in the form of an inexpensive Ford Model T.

It was also an era of significant social change and great fun—so much fun that it was nicknamed "the Roaring Twenties" and "the Jazz Age." Americans were eager to forget the war and enjoy themselves.

A colonial settler stumbles in a drunken stupor. America's love affair with alcohol came to a sudden end in 1920 when the Eighteenth Amendment went into effect, banning the sale of all liquor.

They listened to the radio, danced in nightclubs, and went to see "talkies"—motion pictures with the radical new addition of sound. The younger generation, meanwhile, boldly tested new forms of personal freedom, from the Charleston dance and short skirts to women exercising their new right to vote.

Blowing a Tin Horn

The loose, fun-loving atmosphere of the 1920s was a difficult one in which to sustain a ban on liquor. Nonetheless, the antialcohol forces succeeded, and their tireless efforts resulted in the passage of the Eighteenth Amendment and the Volstead Act.

The advocates who wrote and backed these new laws assumed that a majority of Americans would go along with it. They imagined that most citizens would abide by the law of the land, even if they did not personally approve of it. To the dismay of the drys, however, and despite the efforts of enforcement agents, a vast subculture of illegal drinking evolved across the country. Otherwise law-abiding citizens

As Americans rebelled against Prohibition, speakeasies began to thrive, as this contemporary painting shows.

secretly made home-brewed liquor. Illegal drinking parlors called speakeasies flourished. Criminal gangs and smugglers known as bootleggers made fortunes importing or producing illicit liquor. Law enforcement agencies, meanwhile, were hopelessly underfunded and overwhelmed, and sometimes subject to corruption.

To many observers, America during the 1920s seemed like one long party, during which guests cheerfully ignored the host's rules by getting drunk. Writer Robert Lewis Taylor, looking back in 1966, commented on the sudden and prolonged change in the country. He observed that on the night before Prohibition took effect "the country had gone to bed fairly sober; next morning it awoke, grabbed a red tin New Year's Eve horn and blew it without interruption for [nearly] fourteen years."[3]

The Right to Drink

The flagrant disdain for Prohibition on the part of millions of citizens reflected a conflict deeper than simply the morality of drinking. It touched on a fundamental issue in American life: the role of government in regulating private lives. Many Americans felt that a degree of federal control is justified for the good of the majority. However, others argued that the rights of individual citizens and states should not be limited by the federal government. This latter group argued that the federal government had no right to mandate something as personal—and as trivial, compared with serious crimes—as drinking habits. Historian Norman H. Clark writes: "It was incredible to many people that the federal government, which had thoughtfully left their murders, lynchings, adulteries, discriminations, frauds, and other transgressions [misdeeds] to the disciplines of their state legislatures, would ever take a primary and oppressive interest in what [American citizens] might want to drink."[4]

The conflict over liquor was a long and hard-fought battle. It reached a boiling point in the first decades of the twentieth century.

Dry Versus Wet: The Years Just Before Prohibition

At the start of the twentieth century, two social movements in America formed the overall force behind the push for the prohibition of alcohol. One of these typically appealed to conservative, churchgoing Americans, often concentrated in rural areas. This group generally regarded drunkenness as irreligious and immoral, a personal failing of the wicked. Billy Sunday, the most popular evangelist of the time (and himself a reformed drinker), spoke for many when he thundered, "Liquor is the bloodsucker of humanity; it is God's worst enemy and hell's best friend."[5]

The second movement, more moderate and liberal, was part of a large, loose group of social activists known as Progressives. Progressives were reformers who were generally educated, urban, and middle class. They sought to remedy a wide spectrum of social ills and injustices. Among the causes Progressives championed were women's suffrage (a battle won shortly after Prohibition began), urban slum reform, and the regulation of alcohol (Progressives typically saw alcohol abuse as a correctable social problem rather than a personal failing).

"A Breeding Place of Crime and Violence"

Within these two broad groups, opinions on alcohol varied widely. Very conservative activists, who were commonly called "bone dry," disapproved of liquor absolutely. They wanted to make all forms of it completely illegal at all times. Others were opposed less to milder, fermented forms of alcohol, such as beer and wine, than to whiskey and other distilled, or hard, liquor. Still others saw the question in economic terms, and concerned themselves not with individual drinkers but with regulating the liquor industry and the public drinking houses known as saloons.

Almost all antialcohol activists, bone dry or moderate, agreed on one issue: The biggest problem was the culture of the saloon. Saloons, though long established in American society, generally had terrible reputations. They were considered wicked places where men wasted their families' food money, prostitutes and pickpockets openly plied their trades, and gamblers took advantage of gullible, drunken patrons. Historian Herbert Asbury writes:

As an institution the saloon was a blight and a public stench. It was dingy and dirty, a place of battered furniture, offensive smells . . . and appalling sanitary facilities. It encouraged drunkenness and ignored the law. It corrupted the police, the courts, and the politicians. It was a breeding place of crime and violence, and the hangout of criminals and degenerates of every type.[6]

High-Class or Low-Class

In fact, some saloons did not deserve this lurid reputation. Most cities boasted ornate drinking establishments that resembled legitimate and respectable restaurants. Their customers enjoyed live orchestras, lavish furnishings, elaborate meals, and pleasant outdoor beer gardens. These patrons were decent citizens, and criminals were definitely not welcome.

However, such high-class establishments were in the minority. Most saloons catered to the working and lower classes, and these businesses

Good Templars of the Temperance Society were antialcohol activists who disapproved of saloons and rallied for the regulation of alcohol.

"It Cares for Nothing but Itself"

The famous evangelist Billy Sunday did not mince words when condemning saloons and drinking. This passage, reprinted in Roger A. Bruns's Preacher: Billy Sunday and Big-Time American Evangelism, *is typical of his rhetoric:*

"The saloon will take off the shirt from the back of a shivering man. It will take the coffin from under the dead. It will take the milk from

the breast of the poor mother who is the wife of a drinking man. It will take the crust of bread from the hand of the hungry child. It cares for nothing but itself—for its dirty profits. It will keep your boy out of college. It will make your daughter a prostitute. It will bury your wife in the potter's [pauper's] field. It will send you to hell."

Evangelist Billy Sunday considered alcohol consumption to be irreligious and immoral.

were indeed disreputable and filthy. They offered dismal and depressing atmospheres, and their salty "free lunches" encouraged patrons to linger and drink too much.

Furthermore, saloons often did harbor criminal activity. In addition to admitting prostitutes, pickpockets, and gamblers, they stayed open beyond legal hours, sold liquor to minors, and watered down their drinks. In many cases, saloon owners prospered because they bribed corrupt city officials to look the other way and ignore any illegal activities. Sociologist John M. Barker remarked in 1905, "The saloon has the distinction of standing first in this country in the production of crimes and criminals."[7]

The number of saloons in America grew steadily in the decades before Prohibition. In 1880 there were about 150,000 saloons nationwide. That figure had doubled to nearly 300,000 by 1900. For antiliquor activists, this was an alarming trend.

Immigration and Urbanization

Antiliquor activists also used other arguments to gain support for a ban on alcohol. One argument was tied to widespread prejudice against recent immigrants. Millions of people, mostly Europeans, flocked to America in the late nineteenth and early twentieth centuries. General anti-immigration anxiety led many Americans to complain that these new immigrant groups fostered drunkenness. Wine-loving Italians, whiskey- and beer-loving Irish, beer-loving Germans, and vodka-loving Poles were some of the most numerous immigrant groups, and they came under especially intense criticism.

Another tactic that antialcohol supporters used to bolster their cause was exploiting the deep distrust many Americans felt toward life in the city. During the early twentieth century, as America became increasingly industrialized, the population shifted. Millions of people left their farms and small towns in search of factory work in urban areas. Since most of the country's population, including the new immigrants, was concentrated in these cities, most public drinking took place there; Chicago alone had more saloons than did several Southern states combined. Through antiliquor campaigns, urbanization became linked with drunkenness in the minds of many people.

Most of the industrialists, factory owners, and businessmen who hired these workers also supported prohibition. To them it was typically an issue of money, not morals, because drinking slowed down production. Historian Larry Engelmann notes, "Basically, the economic argument contended that alcohol made the workingman, whether laborer or manager, inefficient and careless. He was likely to make more errors, and errors were likely to cost time, money, profits, and lives."[8]

Some business owners instituted bans on liquor within their own companies. One of America's most famous industrialists, Henry Ford, insisted that every worker in his car factories abstain completely. Ford even sent spies into neighborhoods where workers lived. Any Ford employee caught buying liquor was given a stern warning, and if caught a second time was fired.

State and Local Dry Laws Succeed

A businessman like Ford could control his workplace, but antiliquor activists wanted laws that applied to society in general. This was not easy, however. During the first years of the twentieth century the drys had mixed success with statewide dry laws and no success with national prohibition.

The failure to mount a national campaign was largely the result of political resistance. National prohibition required drafting and passing a constitutional amendment. However, the effort to block this was strong in the nation's capital. Most members of Congress did not support the dry cause, primarily because tackling the sensitive issue of personal freedom—what people could and could not do in their private lives and in their free time—risked alienating voters. Historian Frederick Lewis Allen comments that government generally "was as wary of the prohibition issue as of a large stick of dynamite."[9]

For this reason, prohibition activists had better luck with passing dry laws at the state level. State-level politicians could more readily be persuaded to pass laws controlling only their own areas. Thus, by the turn of the twentieth century, six states had laws prohibiting the manufacture, sale, or consumption of liquor, to varying degrees, within their borders. These varied from total, bone-dry bans to partial bans that allowed, for instance, the consumption of liquor in private homes.

Activists were even more successful with "local option" laws. These laws, which were especially popular in rural areas, were simply versions of statewide bans that applied to smaller districts such as cities or counties. Local option laws were typically sponsored by grassroots organizations such as church groups that could effectively lobby to make their own counties or towns dry.

Because laws varied widely from region to region, the overall effect of state and local option laws was a patchwork quilt of disorganized

Henry Ford had strict alcohol policies for employees of the Ford Motor Company. They were required to abstain from all alcohol, whether at work or not.

The Anti-Saloon League lobbied for passage of the Eighteenth Amendment and the Volstead Act, both of which supported Prohibition.

and contradictory legislation. Nonetheless, the movement toward prohibition gained strength. By 1906 dry laws in one form or another affected more than half of the nation's counties, incorporated towns, townships, and villages. This effectively meant that about 40 percent of the nation's population lived in an area that was to some degree dry.

The Anti-Saloon League

This network of irregular and incomplete dry laws frustrated prohibition advocates. They wanted a series of strong state laws and federal regulations that would eventually lead to a comprehensive national law. One group in particular, the Anti-Saloon League (ASL), led the march to this goal. Founded in Ohio in 1893 and quickly established nationwide, the ASL was the group most directly responsible for the passage of the Eighteenth Amendment and the Volstead Act.

In its policies and actions, the ASL was firmly middle-of-the-road. It was not aligned with any one religious or political group (although much of its support came from several Protestant organizations). Nor were ASL leaders fanatics like Billy Sunday. They were instead calm, professional administrators, fund-raisers, and lawyers. In this regard, the league avoided the appearance of being single-minded and obsessive; instead, it merged its moral stand with a progressive, up-to-date approach to political realities. Historian Thomas R. Pegram notes, "The Anti-Saloon League exhibited the modern face of traditional middle-class moral concern in America."[10]

The ASL did not encourage direct action such as boycotts or harassment of specific bars, breweries, distilleries, or individual drinkers. These targets were too narrowly focused for the league. Instead, it targeted the liquor industry as a whole. It aimed to cripple this industry by pursuing realistic political goals and small but steady gains that gradually restricted the industries ability to operate and make a profit.

The league was content to see changes arrive slowly, over the course of several lawmaking sessions in a given state. "Do not strive after the impossible," the organization's Ohio headquarters advised its branches. "Study local conditions and reach after the attainable."[11] Typical of these objectives were ordinances requiring costly license fees for breweries and laws restricting hours of operations for saloons.

Avoiding the Fanatics

The league's moderate, reasonable approach appealed to many members of the general public. Few people, for instance, disagreed with the group's campaigns to eradicate prostitution and gambling in saloons, or to ban sales of liquor to minors. Many also applauded the league's avoidance of colorful but controversial figures from the radical fringe of the dry spectrum, such as Billy Sunday. Typical of Sunday's extremism were fiery sermons in which he denounced the "damnable, hellish, vile, corrupt, iniquitous [wicked] liquor business. . . . This God-forsaken whisky gang is the worst this side of hell."[12]

Instead, the organization strove to maintain an even-tempered, balanced approach. As one ASL member explained, "There is no need for the business man or church member to make street speeches for temperance [prohibition]. I don't believe in fanatics. They do not accomplish what common sense does."[13]

This approach gave the ASL broad appeal, and the league counted among its supporters a powerful and varied array of individuals and organizations. Supporters included both liberal reformers such as social activist Jane Addams and conservative industrialists such as John D. Rockefeller Sr., Henry Ford, and Pierre du Pont. Norman H. Clark writes that the ASL "became a lens through which the various and diffuse [scattered] energies of Prohibition, evangelical Christianity, feminism, social purity, and political reform could be brought into sharp focus."[14]

The Shadow of Danger

If you believe that the traffic in Alcohol does more harm than good- *help stop it!*

Strengthen America Campaign
Strengthen America Campaign - 105 East Twenty Second Street, New York City, N.Y.

This Prohibition-era poster portrays the evils of alcohol.

"The Poor Man's Club"

Thomas R. Pegram, in Battling Demon Rum: The Struggle for a Dry America, *describes the important role old-fashioned saloons played in the lives of working-class and lower-class men:*

"The most important function of the urban, working-class saloon, observers agreed, was as 'the poor man's club.' Working-class men had no access to the well-appointed hotel bars and exclusive clubs that offered recreation to salaried and professional men. For men who worked in sweaty, often dangerous jobs and lived in crowded, stuffy tenements, the saloon beckoned as a warm, well-lit, pleasant refuge for relaxation and masculine companionship. Men played cards, read newspapers, discussed politics, sports, and theology in saloons. Many barrooms provided pool tables or pianos; occasionally there was an attached gymnasium, bowling alley, or handball court."

Standing Right or Wrong

One of the ASL's most effective tools was propaganda. At its peak, the organization's presses produced forty tons of printed material each month. These publications, which were distributed widely across the country, emphasized the low taxes, peaceful politics, and booming economies that would surely result from a saloon-free America.

This literature, and the frequent lectures and rallies the ASL held, were designed to enhance its most powerful weapon: the organization of registered voters into specific voting groups. This lobbying was done primarily through church organizations. Once voters were united behind the ASL's cause, the league worked hard to persuade them to contact their elected officials and voice their opinions.

The ASL also urged its supporters to vote for certain politicians who had declared themselves dry. Voters, the ASL reasoned, had the ability to influence incumbent politicians to adopt dry standards, or to elect others who would.

For politicians who wanted to cultivate the dry vote, the endorsement of the ASL was crucial. The league promised the support of its millions of voters to any politician who backed its measures, regardless of the politician's party affiliation. In fact, the ASL actively encouraged its members to vote across party lines. The league's official policy statement urged supporters to "forsake their party in at least one campaign, and vote for a man who is personally distasteful to them, who does not belong to their church and their lodge, and who stands right, instead of a man on their own party ticket who perhaps belongs to their church, belongs, perhaps, to all their lodges, and is a personal friend, but who stands wrong."[15]

The Webb-Kenyon Act

By 1913 the ASL had achieved several notable successes. It had guided the passage of dry laws in several states. Its support was crucial in passing several national measures as well, including a ban on liquor sales on military bases and greater enforcement of alcohol laws on Indian reservations.

However, the league had not yet made an official push for national prohibition. In fact, the organization had avoided the issue for years because it did not yet have enough influence in Congress to pass a national law. Typical of its official attitude was a 1906 statement in which the league prudently noted that it approved of prohibition "in those states which have or are ready for such laws."[16] This statement specifically avoided the uncertain issue of a national ban on alcohol.

However, in 1913 the league scored its most significant victory yet, one that gave ASL leaders enough confidence to pick up the banner of national prohibition. This victory was the passage of the Webb-Kenyon Act.

Webb-Kenyon, coauthored by Senators William Webb, a Democrat, and William Kenyon, a Republican, concerned the interstate transport of alcohol, an issue that came under federal jurisdiction and could not be decided by individual states. The act barred the importation of liquor into any state if the alcohol was to be used in violation of any existing law of that state.

The law was carefully worded to make it seem that Webb-Kenyon was a states' rights bill, emphasizing the power of individual states over federal control. It was worded this way because the league felt that an emphasis on states' rights would make the bill acceptable to politicians who were passionate about keeping the power of the federal government in check.

"The First Shot"

The ASL was correct in that assumption. Webb-Kenyon was popular even with some politicians who otherwise opposed prohibition. Clark writes, "It seemed to be the kind of noble, if harmless, statement one expected from Progressives and idealists, and on that basis some wets voted for it."[17] The bill was bland enough to satisfy antiprohibition politicians, but powerful enough to give the ASL a significant gain.

Drys in the Washington State House of Representatives supported Prohibition. States across the nation passed dry laws.

Webb-Kenyon was vetoed by President William Howard Taft, who felt that the measure was both repressive and unconstitutional. However, Congress overrode his veto, and after legal challenges the Supreme Court upheld the bill as constitutionally sound.

The passage of Webb-Kenyon demonstrated that the Anti-Saloon League could wield significant power in the national government. Furthermore, Congress at the time had a significant number of dry politicians. A formal push for national prohibition seemed possible.

ASL officials sensed that the time was right, and in 1913 put the matter to a vote at the annual meeting of the league's national board of trustees. The vote was unanimous; the ASL would push for a national ban on alcohol. The ASL's chief lawyer and driving force, an Ohio-born attorney named Wayne Wheeler, later recalled the scene when the decision was made: "For a moment there was silence, deep and tense. Then the convention cut loose. With a roar as wild as the raging storm outside [the crowd] jumped to its feet and yelled approval. The first shot in the Eighteenth Amendment had been fired."[18]

Lobbying

League officials then got down to work. They realized that the key to their success was in the upcoming 1914 elections. They needed to elect or return as many dry politicians as possible to Congress.

To accomplish this, the league blanketed the country with litera-ture, lobbied politicians already in Washington, and dispersed about fifty thousand well-trained speakers, volunteers, and staffers across America to conduct lectures and door-to-door campaigns and other-wise spread the word. History professor Thomas R. Pegram writes, "During 1914 League speakers crisscrossed the country, League pe-titions and telegrams piled up on the desks of elected officials, and the League spent a record $2.5 million."[19]

After mobilizing these forces, late in 1913 the league formally pre-sented its petition to Congress. This resolution, as it was called, was not a constitutional amendment; instead, it was a formal proclamation calling for the creation of such an amendment. Four thousand sup-porters gathered in Washington, D.C., and, decorated with the league's symbol of white ribbons, marched down Pennsylvania Av-enue to the Capitol building.

There they presented the resolution to two longtime dry advocates, Senator Morris Sheppard of Texas and Representative Richmond P. Hobson of Alabama. The two had already agreed to introduce the reso-lution in their respective houses in Congress.

The Hobson-Sheppard Resolution

The Hobson-Sheppard Resolution, as the petition became known, was carefully worded. It sought to bar the manufacture and sale of liquor, but not its use. This distinction was a compromise, made as a concession to wet politicians, that kept Hobson-Sheppard from cre-ating a "bone-dry" law.

At the time, only a handful of states were already completely dry. Most states that already had some dry laws distinguished the regulation of the liquor industry from the regulation of personal con-sumption; typically, the state laws allowed individuals to import or make alcohol for personal use. Hobson-Sheppard sought to do the same thing nationally.

The resolution did not pass either house of Congress. Nonetheless, the bill achieved a solid yes vote, enough to encourage the league to continue its work. Even better signs, from the ASL perspective, were the outcomes of the 1914 and 1916 elections. In 1914, several new dry senators were elected. This gave antiliquor activists a clear majority in the Senate.

The House of Representatives, however, was still short of a dry ma-jority. The ASL therefore began preparing for the next election in 1916, when they hoped to achieve this goal. Wayne Wheeler recalled, "All the energy we put into the 1914 election boiled and bubbled with hotter fire in the campaign of 1916."[20]

Morris Sheppard (left), a Texas senator, and Richmond P. Hobson, an Alabama representative, introduced the Hobson-Sheppard Resolution, a petition to ban alcohol.

The result of this effort was a triumph that surpassed even the ASL's expectations. Another four states passed dry laws in 1916, and a majority of dry politicians were elected or returned to both the House and the Senate.

National prohibition now appeared inevitable. "It seemed then certain," Clark writes, "that the dry Congress would raise the spirit of state Prohibition laws to the level of federal legislation, that the movement of a hundred years—the Antiliquor Movement, like the Antislave Movement—would indeed reach its fulfillment in the federal Constitution."[21]

Wartime

However, the push for prohibition and other domestic affairs were interrupted in 1917 by U.S. involvement in World War I. The bloody conflict had been raging in Europe since 1914, pitting Germany and the Central Powers against England, France, and other Allies. Until 1917 the United States maintained its neutrality, though American sympathies lay with the Allies. When the threat of German submarine warfare against American ships grew, however, President Woodrow Wilson called Congress into special session to formally request the authority to declare war on Germany. Congress agreed and America entered the battle in April 1917.

The decision affected antiliquor activists for the better as well as for the worse. In some ways the war hindered the prohibitionist cause. Until the conflict ended late in 1919 prohibition took a back seat to more urgent concerns, such as the mobilization of military forces. However, some historians feel that the Eighteenth Amendment might never have been approved at all if it had not been for the war.

One way the war helped the antiliquor cause was that it stressed the importance of conserving the nation's resources, especially for food production. The most important example of this was President Wilson's desire to regulate the production of grain. He wanted America's grain supplies to be used to feed troops and civilians, rather than for brewing. Dry advocates readily agreed and adopted the motto "Shall the many have food, or the few have drink?"[22]

President Woodrow Wilson addresses Congress in 1917 about America's involvement in World War I. America's entry into the war both hindered and helped the prohibition cause.

Anti-German Sentiment

Wartime also gave prohibition advocates an additional weapon: a widespread mistrust and hatred of Germans and all things German. Although anti-immigrant sentiment in general was still strong, in 1917 the focus shifted specifically onto this enemy nationality.

The dislike for German things included beer; German immigrants had brought with them to America their centuries-old tradition of brewing and beer drinking as a fundamental social custom. Anti-German sentiment was especially strong in cities such as Milwaukee, Wisconsin, and Cincinnati, Ohio, where large German American communities and breweries flourished.

During the war, all things German, including brewing companies, came under suspicion. Some people considered the very act of drinking a beer to be somehow unpatriotic. The ASL did not shrink from using this anti-German sentiment for its own purposes. As Behr writes, "[Wayne] Wheeler and his assistants lost no time reminding Americans that the brewing interests were almost all in German hands, and that at some brewers' meetings the very language used was German."[23]

Largely as a result of ASL criticism, Germans and German breweries came under attack. Business for breweries owned by German Americans dropped steeply. The United States Brewers Association, a group of mostly German Americans, was repeatedly and publicly accused of anti-American activity, while large brewing companies, such as Pabst and Schlitz, were denounced as traitorous.

The Wartime Prohibition Act

Antiliquor forces continued to press their cause as the war dragged on throughout 1917 and 1918. Their next major success came in November 1918, the same month in which the signing of an armistice marked the end of the long war. That month, Congress passed a bill that had been in the works for some time: a temporary Wartime Prohibition Act.

In the name of emergency conservation, the Wartime Prohibition Act banned the manufacture of all beer and wine as of May 1919. It also prohibited the sale of all intoxicating beverages beginning in June 1919. The ban was to last until America's armed forces were returned to peacetime status, a process called demobilization, because Congress felt that the chaotic procedure of demobilization was essentially part of the war.

President Wilson vetoed the bill. He deemed it unconstitutional and unnecessary. Since the actual fighting was over, he reasoned, there was no more need to conserve grain. However, Congress overrode his veto and passed the law.

Kegs of beer are dumped into Lake Michigan from Chicago docks. The Wartime Prohibition Act banned all manufacture and sale of beer and wine.

The Wartime Prohibition Act passed with so little opposition because few politicians wanted to be perceived as unpatriotic. They felt that a vote against the bill would brand them as working against the patriotic Anti-Saloon League and America's best interests. One newspaper at the time, remarking on Congress's override of Wilson's veto, commented, "The average member of Congress is more afraid of the Anti-Saloon League than he is even of the President of the United States."[24]

On the Verge of Prohibition

ASL supporters, of course, were elated by the passage of the Wartime Prohibition Act. It effectively created a national prohibition with no firm end date. At the league's Worldwide Prohibition Congress in Columbus, Ohio, only days after the war ended, Reverend Sam Small thundered that he and his colleagues were beating the devil: "From the Great Lakes to the Gulf a militant majority of American people are crucifying that beastly, bloated bastard of Beelzebub, the liquor traffic."[25]

The long years of work for the supporters of national prohibition were about to pay off. A second attempt at creating a constitutional amendment was already in the works, and it would succeed.

John Barleycorn Is Dead: Prohibition Becomes Law

Only one month after America entered World War I in 1917, the ASL had introduced to Congress a successor to Hobson-Sheppard. The new resolution in time became the Eighteenth Amendment and banned liquor nationally. The joint resolution was officially unrelated to the Wartime Prohibition Act—they were separate laws, passing through Congress at different times—but it served much the same purpose. In effect, the Wartime Prohibition Act created a temporary national prohibition until a proposed constitutional amendment could be ratified by the individual states.

When this second prohibition resolution was put to a vote in Congress in 1917, it was quickly approved by the required two-thirds majority. It passed the Senate by a vote of 65-20, while a majority of 282-128 approved it in the House of Representatives. The measure was approved by the Senate after just thirteen hours of debate. The House took even less time.

This was an astonishingly short period of time for such an important measure. Normally controversial laws spend months or even years in committee and prolonged debate follows. In this case, however, the nation's lawmakers were ready for a ban on liquor. Writing in 1931, author Frederick Lewis Allen noted, "Nothing in recent American history is more extraordinary, as one looks back from the nineteen-thirties, than the ease with which—after generations of uphill fighting by the drys—prohibition was finally written upon the statute-books. The country accepted it not only willingly, but almost absent-mindedly."[26]

The nation's dry forces, of course, were thrilled. Billy Sunday staged a mock funeral service for "John Barleycorn," a nickname for liquor. Before a cheering crowd, a troupe of mimes impersonating drunkards and devils accompanied a twenty-foot coffin as Sunday roared, "We will turn our prisons into factories! Men will walk upright now, women will smile, and the children will laugh. Hell will be forever for rent!"[27]

A Compromise Resolution

The Eighteenth Amendment was not designed to create a bone-dry nation. Instead, it was a classic example of compromise, filled with

Clarence Darrow (right) and Wayne Wheeler of the Anti-Saloon League after a Prohibition debate.

trade-offs that were acceptable to wet and dry politicians alike. (Much of the proposed amendment's language had been crafted by Wayne Wheeler, a master of political compromise.) The result was a law that people on both sides of the debate called "moist" or "damp"—in other words, neither very wet nor very dry.

Compromise resolutions, by their very nature, are inevitably weaker than hard-liners on either side might want. This is because each side must soften its position and accept trade-offs that make the measure acceptable to all concerned. Nonetheless, the language of the 1917 resolution was bolder than that of the failed Hobson-Sheppard Resolution of 1914.

Hobson-Sheppard had sought to forbid only the manufacture and shipment of intoxicating liquor. The new version went further. It barred "the manufacture, sale, or transportation of intoxicating liquors . . . for beverage purposes."[28] This was a subtle but important distinction. The newer measure prohibited not just the manufacture and transportation of alcohol, but its sale as well. The proposed amendment thus went beyond most politicians'—and the ASL's—usual reluctance to interfere with individual rights. Later, this hard-line stance would be significantly weakened by the Volstead Act.

When Is a Drink Intoxicating?

Another key compromise concerned the use of the phrase "intoxicating liquors." Though hard-line prohibitionists objected, Congress had agreed on the wording "intoxicating liquors" without specifying an alcohol level.

This compromise was made because Wheeler and his colleagues in government knew that, even after Congress had approved the amendment, the legislatures of the individual states would have to ratify it before it could become law. The amendment's backers worried that some politicians would not support a hard-line law that clearly outlawed all forms of alcoholic drink at every level. According to Norman H. Clark, the politicians knew "full well that a radical, bone-dry

26

amendment, in the absence of enough bone-dry, radical states, would never achieve ratificaton."[29]

Instead, the resolution left open the question of exactly what constituted an alcoholic drink and how it qualified as intoxicating. This was not an easily answered question. Many wets and even a few moderate

Wheeler and Volstead

Although he preferred to stay out of the public eye, Wayne Wheeler was the primary force behind the Eighteenth Amendment and the Volstead Act. As chief lawyer for the Anti-Saloon League, he conceived and drafted large sections of both pieces of legislation. It was typical of his behind-the-scenes style, however, that few people know his name. Instead, a man who did not oppose alcohol, Representative Andrew J. Volstead, gave his name to the law enforcing Prohibition.

Wheeler was a brilliant, charismatic, and tireless campaigner for Prohibition all his adult life. Born in 1869, he was the fourth of nine children of an Ohio cattle dealer and farmer. Wheeler claimed to have turned against alcohol after a boyhood incident in which a drunken, pitchfork-wielding neighbor wounded him.

While Wheeler was attending Oberlin College in Ohio, an ASL executive recruited him to lecture and organize voters. Wheeler remained with the league for the rest of his life. Attending law school while working for the league, he became its in-house attorney and later boasted that he lost only ten of the three thousand cases he argued on behalf of the ASL.

Moving to Washington, D.C., as the organization's legislative superintendent, or chief lobbyist, Wheeler became a force in national politics. He also kept close tabs on which public officials supported his cause.

Andrew J. Volstead was not one of them. Although he was quiet, reserved, and religious, he was never a hard-core advocate of Prohibition. Born in 1860, Volstead was a county attorney as well as city attorney and mayor in rural Minnesota before being elected to the U.S. House of Representatives. As a county attorney in a dry state, Volstead prosecuted many cases involving illegal liquor, but he did so because it was his job, not because of personal beliefs. Later, as chairman of the House Judiciary Committee, it became Volstead's responsibility to introduce the act that bore his name and legislated Prohibition enforcement.

drys were of the opinion that light forms of liquor, such as wine and beer, were not strictly intoxicating. The wording of the new bill left them wondering: At what alcoholic content does a drink become intoxicating?

This ambiguity had also been part of the temporary Wartime Prohibition Act. Although that law had not precisely defined an intoxicating level of alcohol, it had approved a 2.75 percent "near beer" for wartime use. The framers of the Eighteenth Amendment now debated adopting that same alcohol level or some other higher or lower level. Congress could not agree on an acceptable level, however, and for the time being the question was left open.

A Short Time Frame

One of the most important concessions to wet supporters concerned the time frame for states to ratify the amendment. According to the Constitution, in order to become law, a proposed amendment required ratification by three-fourths of the states; Congress had the ability to set a time limit for this to occur. The Eighteenth Amendment was given a ratification limit of seven years.

This was an extremely short time period for a law addressing such a contentious issue. Many wet politicians felt confident that the relatively brief period would prevent the amendment from being approved by enough states. Prohibition was so controversial, they reasoned, that enough states would still be arguing about it when the deadline arrived.

Dry politicians and ASL officials also thought ratification would take a long time. They assumed that they had an uphill battle involving years of intense lobbying in each state before a three-quarters majority could be achieved. After all, fourteen states had already refused to pass state prohibition laws, and there was no reason to think that they would approve national prohibition. Even the states that were already dry might balk at a federally mandated law.

Therefore, immediately after the joint resolution passed through Congress, ASL organizations in every state went to work. Supporters inundated state leaders with telegrams and letters, urging approval of the proposed amendment. They held marches and organized rallies. They passed out literature to friends and neighbors, and in churches and Sunday schools they sang antiliquor songs; typical was "Onward, Temperance Soldiers," sung to the tune of "Onward, Christian Soldiers."

An Easy Victory

The efficient organization and strong lobbying tactics on the part of the state-level ASL branches proved extremely effective. Despite the

Prohibitionists march on the capital seeking a Prohibition amendment to the Constitution. Thirty-six states ratified the amendment before it was adopted into the Constitution.

dire predictions, the necessary majority of states easily approved the amendment in record time. This speed surprised even the most ardent drys. "We thought it would take three or four years to get the amendment ratified," an ASL official remarked at the time. "Instead, . . . the thing's becoming as simple as 'A.B.C.'"[30]

In January 1918, just one month after Congress approved the amendment, Mississippi became the first state to ratify it. One year later, in January 1919, Nebraska became the thirty-sixth state to do so, achieving the necessary three-fourths majority. Eventually, all but two states approved the measure. (Connecticut and Rhode Island did not.) The *New York Tribune* commented that the amendment's speedy progress was "as if a sailing ship on a windless ocean were sweeping ahead, propelled by some invisible force."[31] The *New York Times* added wryly that joining the antiliquor side was apparently becoming chic: "Prohibition seems to be the fashion, just as drinking once was."[32]

On January 29, 1919, the secretary of state announced that on January 16 the necessary thirty-six states had ratified the amendment. The Eighteenth Amendment to the Constitution was formally adopted, retroactive to the day the last state had approved it. According to the terms of the amendment, it was to go into effect exactly one year later, on January 17, 1920.

The Volstead Act

In its entirety, the Eighteenth Amendment is only three sentences long. Thus, more detailed laws were needed to clarify the amendment's meaning and to create specific guidelines for its enforcement. To this end, the National Prohibition Act was introduced in Congress in May 1919. This bill was popularly called the Volstead Act, after Andrew Volstead, the Minnesota representative who sponsored it. After only about three months of debate, the House passed the Volstead Act by an overwhelming majority. Senate approval quickly followed.

President Wilson, however, vetoed the act. Although he was personally concerned about the negative effects of drinking, he disapproved of enforced prohibition on ethical grounds. Wilson believed that it was morally wrong to impose mandatory dry laws on all citizens.

Wilson also thought that the measure was unconstitutional. In other words, he did not believe that the imposition of abstinence on all Americans could stand up to the intense analysis required of constitutional law. He felt that if prohibition were to be carried out at all, it should be done by means other than a constitutional amendment.

However, Congress overrode the president's veto, and the Volstead Act became law. It went into effect on October 10, 1919, replacing state dry laws already in force.

Title II

The Volstead Act included three parts, called titles. Title I stipulated that the commissioner of the Internal Revenue Bureau (later the In-

Anti-prohibition demonstrators march in a parade. President Wilson vetoed the Eighteenth Amendment but the veto was overridden.

ternal Revenue Service) was to carry out enforcement of Prohibition. Title I also specified a maximum legal alcohol content of 0.5 percent. This strict standard, which surprised many moderate observers, was one point on which hard-line prohibitionists prevailed. Any liquor containing more than 0.5 percent alcohol was now to be considered intoxicating and illegal. Title III of the act established guidelines for government control of industrial alcohol, a product that was vital to America's rapidly growing chemical industry.

Title II was the act's most important section. This part of the law laid out the rules by which Prohibition would be enforced. Title II specifically allowed the use of certain kinds of alcohol for medical or religious purposes. However, it banned liquor advertising and forbade the use or sale of any product that might lead to the manufacture of alcohol.

Title II further specified measures for punishing those who broke the law. Anyone who manufactured, transported, or sold illegal liquor was subject to fines of up to one thousand dollars (a large amount of money at the time) and six months of jail for a first offense. Second or third violations were punishable with fines up to ten thousand dollars and five years in jail. Finally, Title II authorized the creation of a government agency called the Prohibition Unit (later renamed the Prohibition Bureau). This agency was responsible for enforcing the new laws.

Title II specified what the new agency could and could not do. For instance, under a subsection of Title II known as the Padlock Law, bureau agents could close, for up to one year, a building that housed any operation that illegally manufactured or sold liquor. Thus, if an illegal still was found in the basement of an apartment building, the entire building could be seized. Bureau agents also had the authority to destroy confiscated liquor and to seize and sell any cars, boats, airplanes, or other vehicles used by smugglers.

Exemptions

Some sections of the Volstead Act limited the range of the Prohibition Bureau's activities. For instance, the bureau could not search private homes unless it could prove that illegal liquor was being sold within. Also, certain kinds of alcohol were exempt from the ban under certain conditions. These sections of the law were the result of compromises worked out to avoid political controversy or to create legal exemptions for certain industries and activities. For instance, the Jewish and Roman Catholic religions require the use of wine for certain holidays and ceremonies. Lawmakers were eager to avoid accusations of obstructing religious freedom. Thus, they created a permit process that allowed the use of sacramental wines for religious celebrations and observances.

What Could and Could Not Be Done

The day before Prohibition went into effect, the New York Daily News *published a list of guidelines intepreting the new law for the public. It is reprinted in Edward Behr's* Prohibition: Thirteen Years That Changed America.

"You may drink intoxicating liquor in your own home or in the home of a friend when you are a bona fide [genuine] guest.

You may buy intoxicating liquor on a bona fide medical prescription of a doctor. A pint can be bought every ten days.

You may consider any place you live permanently as your home. If you have more than one home, you may keep a stock of liquor in each.

You may keep liquor in any storage room or club locker, provided the storage place is for the exclusive use of yourself, family or bona fide friends.

You may get a permit to move liquor when you change your residence.

You may manufacture, sell or transport liquor for non-beverage or sacramental purposes provided you obtain a Government permit.

You cannot carry a hip flask.

You cannot give away or receive a bottle of liquor as a gift.

You cannot take liquor to hotels or restaurants and drink it in the public dining rooms.

You cannot buy or sell formulas or recipes for homemade liquors.

You cannot ship liquor for beverage use.

You cannot manufacture anything above one half of one percent [liquor strength] in your home.

You cannot store liquor in any place except your own home.

You cannot display liquor signs or advertisements on your premises.

You cannot remove reserve stocks from storage."

Also, licensed physicians were allowed to prescribe liquor for medicinal purposes, although prescriptions were limited to a pint per patient within a ten-day period. Furthermore, the Volstead Act allowed the use of alcohol in the manufacture of certain food products, including flavoring extracts, syrups, cider, and vinegar.

The Volstead Act's most important exemption, however, concerned the personal use of liquor at home. Possession and use of liquor was legal in private residences, but only if it was for the personal use of the homeowner, his family, or guests. This contradictory loophole made it legal to serve alcohol in one's home, though it was not legal to make, transport, or buy it.

The League Maintains Control

The Anti-Saloon League and its leader, Wayne Wheeler, had been primary forces in framing both the Eighteenth Amendment and the Volstead Act. Not surprisingly, the league and Wheeler wanted to ensure themselves a direct hand in the administration and enforcement of Prohibition.

One way they did this was to wield considerable power over who received jobs as Prohibition Bureau agents. The league managed to set hiring guidelines without regard to merit, competence, or prior experience. One's political loyalties became the only criteria for appointment as an agent. This allowed the league to maintain control over appointees.

Another way the ASL exerted its influence concerned the placement of the Prohibition Bureau within the government bureaucracy. Thanks to manipulation by Wheeler, the bureau did not become part of the Justice Department, where other law enforcement agencies were located. Instead, it was placed within the Internal Revenue Bureau, which was itself part of the Treasury Department.

Wheeler's rationale was that because Internal Revenue already had alcohol-related duties through enforcing an existing tax on liquor, a system for dealing with Prohibition was already in place. However, the tax collection agency had few agents and large case loads. As a result, the already overworked Internal Revenue commissioner readily agreed when Wheeler suggested that he hand over many of the new bureau's duties to league officials. Thomas R. Pegram notes, "As long as the exhausted Internal Revenue Service was responsible for prohibition enforcement, the League had access to power and authority."[33]

Wheeler Takes the Wheel

Wheeler used his influence yet again when it came to choosing someone to head the new bureau. The first Prohibition commissioner, John F. Kramer, was appointed by President Wilson, a Democrat. Wheeler disliked Kramer, who was concerned about the difficulty of enforcing Prohibition. Wheeler wanted to find someone else to head the bureau, someone who echoed his own claims that Prohibition would be simple to enforce and would require only a minimum amount of money.

His chance came in 1921, when a sympathetic Republican president, Warren G. Harding, replaced Wilson. Wheeler and the new president decided to replace Kramer. Their choice was a little-known Ohio newspaper editor named Roy A. Haynes, whose attitude was more in keeping with Wheeler's than the more pragmatic Kramer's had been.

Wheeler enjoyed wielding power behind the scenes in this way, and he continued to influence the nation's alcohol ban for years. Pegram writes that from 1919 until his death from a heart attack in 1927, Wheeler was "the most influential private citizen in the United States in matters concerning prohibition."[34] The *Cincinnati Enquirer*, which was not generally sympathetic to Wheeler, went further, calling him "the strongest political force of his day."[35]

Prohibition Begins

In drafting the Prohibition laws, Wheeler and his colleagues had stipulated a one-year grace period between the date of ratification and the start of Prohibition. This delay served several purposes. First, it gave authorities time to set up ways to enforce the new law. It also gave saloon keepers, brewers, and others in the liquor business time to close down their businesses and find new work.

Furthermore, it allowed people who still wanted to drink time in which to buy and stockpile supplies of existing liquor, which would still be legal to own even after it became illegal to sell any alcohol. Norman H. Clark notes that the grace period allowed those with means to stock large supplies of liquor: "This exclusion allowed a good many wealthy people the comfort of avoiding the great thirst without having to fight the government or the ASL."[36]

In the months leading up to January 1920, many distilleries, hotels, nightclubs, and individuals stockpiled liquor or stored it abroad. (The Bahamas was a popular storage location, and after 1920 it became a favorite site from which to smuggle illegal liquor into America.) Many people rented storage space in warehouses or even safe deposit boxes. Posters bearing an image of Uncle Sam appeared all over America, urging drinkers to "Buy now. Uncle Sam will ENFORCE prohibition!"[37]

Then, two days before Prohibition went into effect, a federal judge threw everyone who was stockpiling liquor into confusion. For unknown reasons, he decreed that after January 17 all liquor stocks outside private homes would constitute a violation of the law. In response, millions of people all across America frantically carted liquor stashes from various locations to their homes. The *New York Evening Post* reported a rush to "hire trucks or baby carriages or anything else on wheels,"[38] while the *San Francisco Chronicle* reported seeing "fair ladies [sitting] in limousines behind alluring barricades of cases."[39]

When the last night of legal liquor finally arrived, drinkers across the country made the most of it. In Cincinnati, the German American

President Harding signs the Volstead Act. It included a loophole that allowed alcohol in private residences for personal use.

Alliance, patriotically renamed the Citizens' League, held a melancholy beer festival. A lavish private party in a New York hotel, meanwhile, featured all-black decorations, drinks served in black glasses, guests and servers dressed in black, a black-clad orchestra playing sad songs, and a black coffin filled with black bottles.

John Barleycorn's Last Breath

On January 17, 1920, at midnight, America officially went dry. The *New York Morning World* commented on that day, "Tonight's the night. Poor old John Barleycorn, doomed to breathe his last at midnight, is dying game [bravely]. It looks as if his last breath will be strong enough."[40] The *New York Times* put it more succinctly the next morning: "JOHN BARLEYCORN DIED PEACEFULLY AT THE TOLL OF 12."[41]

For some, the end of legal drinking was a joyous occasion; for others, it was sad. In either case, it was not the cataclysmic event that some had predicted. The year-long grace period, coupled with the years of wartime restrictions (and years of dryness in many states, towns, and cities) had prepared Americans for the change, whether they were devoted drinkers, passionate drys, or simply indifferent. As Clark notes, "The dry morning of January 17 brought no national trauma."[42] Prohibition was now the law of the land.

CHAPTER 3 The Roots of Temperance in America

Throughout America's history, some people have drunk liquor and others have opposed it. By the time Prohibition arrived in 1920, the issue had been passionately debated in the country for more than a century.

A Suitable Alternative

Drinking in America began with the early colonists. When one of the ships bringing Puritan settlers to Massachusetts Bay arrived in 1630, its cargo included 10,000 gallons of beer, 120 hogs heads of malt for brewing more beer, and 12 gallons of hard liquor. These were just the community's stores; each family also had its own supply of liquor and brewing supplies and equipment.

These stores were needed because most adults in the colonies drank liquor regularly. It was, in many ways, the only agreeable beverage around. Water from rivers and primitive wells often tasted bad and sometimes made people sick. Milk spoiled quickly, and coffee and tea were expensive imported items.

Alcohol, however, was a suitable alternative. Whiskey warmed a body during cold winters, and ale and hard cider refreshed on a hot afternoon. Also, whiskey, ale, and cider kept well and were cheap to make, since ingredients such as corn and apples were readily available. Furthermore, rum, although imported from the Caribbean colonies, was readily available and nearly as cheap as homemade liquor.

"A Semiperpetual Haze"

Typically, a man drank beer or ale with breakfast and lunch. (As president, for example, James Madison customarily downed a pint of ale or cider with breakfast.) Men also often drank shots of rum at "grog time"—midmorning and midafternoon—and more shots of whiskey at various other times during the day. Women also drank alcoholic beverages, although generally less frequently and vigorously. As historian Jack S. Blocker puts it, "Virtually everyone drank virtually all the time."[43]

Furthermore, alcohol, especially whiskey, was commonly used for its medicinal properties. In those days of primitive medicine before anesthetics, it was often the only painkilling remedy available. Writer Henry Lee notes, "For toothache, broken leg, common cold, pneumonia, snakebite, scalp wound or the subtler miseries now treated by the psychiatrists, there was only one obvious relief."[44] Even babies were commonly given rum to keep them pacified.

Such practices extended well into the first decades of American independence. Edward Behr notes: "Eighteenth-century Americans, whether rich or poor, slaves or free men and women, appear to have gone through life in a semiperpetual alcoholic haze."[45]

Binding Society Together

Social drinking also played an important role in binding the settlers into a cohesive group that could face their new home's raw and often intimidating environment. As America became more settled, liquor continued to serve this same social purpose.

Alcohol was the drink of choice for American colonists. It kept longer than other beverages, was cheaper, and was easy to make.

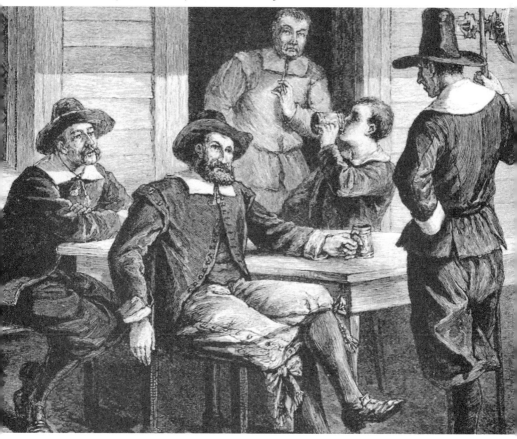

Gatherings such as weddings, funerals, harvests, and barn building parties brought neighbors together—and served as opportunities for communal, socially approved drinking. For instance, guests at the ordination of the Reverend Edwin Jackson of Woburn, Massachusetts, consumed six and a half barrels of hard cider, two gallons of brandy, four gallons of rum, and twenty-five gallons of wine. Such celebrations were frequent in all levels of society. Historian Roger A. Bruns points out: "From rural farmhouses to city taverns, from isolated mountain cabins to the fine tables of Washington's Mt. Vernon, they drank."[46]

Alcohol was even connected with the political process, because drinking houses were routinely used as polling places and for official meetings. Moreover, liquor was considered a natural, even necessary, campaign expense and cost of doing business. For instance, when running for a seat in the House of Burgesses in Virginia in 1758, George Washington spent most of his campaign budget on alcohol for voters on election day. Court sessions, meanwhile, routinely became drinking sessions; the liquor consumed by a judge and jury was considered a legitimate court expense.

Early Voices of Temperance

Of course, not everyone in early America approved of unlimited alcohol consumption. Typical of these was the famous Puritan preacher Increase Mather. He tolerated moderate drinking, noting the many biblical references to the joys and comfort alcohol could bring. But he warned sternly against abusing it. Mather said, "Wine is from God but the drunkard is from the devil."[47]

Many physicians also criticized excessive drinking. One who expressed this opinion was Dr. Benjamin Rush, the most prominent doctor in America after the Revolutionary War. Rush, a Philadelphian, was the former surgeon-general of the Continental Army, a member of the Continental Congress, and a signer of the Declaration of Independence. Along with other prominent early Americans, including Thomas Jefferson, Rush regarded alcohol abuse as a national disease. In his widely read pamphlet "An Inquiry into the Effects of Ardent Spirits upon the Human Body and Mind," Rush concluded that "poverty and misery, crimes and infamy, diseases and death, are all the natural and usual consequences of the intemperate [unrestrained] use of ardent spirits [hard liquor]."[48]

The key words for Rush in this phrase were "intemperate" and "ardent spirits." Like Increase Mather and others, Rush did not support complete abstention. He recommended instead the replacement of hard liquor with moderate amounts of wine, cider, and beer, which he believed led to cheerful and wholesome social interaction.

Because of their Puritan beliefs, Pilgrims were early American advocates of temperance.

Rush even considered these lighter drinks to be patriotic. Rush wrote that they were "invaluable FEDERAL liquors" which served America well by making people cheerful and pleasant, as opposed to what he called "Antifederal" or un-American hard liquor, "companions of all those vices that are calculated to dishonor and enslave our country."[49]

Alcohol and Politics

Despite the efforts of advocates for moderation such as Rush, alcohol use was so ingrained in American life that arguments for personal temperance (restraint or abstention) had little effect in the years after the Revolutionary War. Calls for change through legislation similarly met with no significant success.

One reason politicians avoided curbing America's drinking habits was that alcohol was a significant source of money for the government. Shortly after the Revolutionary War, government authorities had begun taxing liquor, especially rum and whiskey, to raise much-needed revenue for the treasury.

In addition, many politicians recognized that simply passing laws would have little effect on notoriously independent-minded Americans. As Boston congressman Fisher Ames noted in 1788, "If any man supposes that a mere law can turn the taste of a people from ardent spirits to malt liquors, he has a most romantic notion of legislative power."[50]

Ten Nights in a Bar Room

The government thus did avoid the issue, but concerned citizens did not. During the early nineteenth century, a number of temperance organizations formed. By 1835 an estimated 1.5 million Americans (out of about 14.7 million) belonged to roughly eight thousand temperance organizations. Most of these were ineffective and short-lived. In 1823 the *Boston Recorder* noted, "Their influence was gone even sooner than their names." [51]

Some, however, proved to be long lasting and surprisingly effective. The largest of these was the American Temperance Society (ATS), founded in 1826. Largely because of this organization, alcohol con-

Temperance organizations sprang up throughout the nineteenth century, as this poster shows.

sumption in America dropped early in the nineteenth century, from a peak average of four gallons per person annually in 1830 to two gallons in 1840.

Early temperance societies such as the ATS spread their message in many ways. Public lectures and sermons, along with books, newspapers, and pamphlets, were popular methods. Typical of the literature they promoted was a novel that was a best-seller in 1850, *Ten Nights in a Bar Room and What I Saw There*. This story, about a young man with a bright future whose alcoholism costs him his job and family before he sees the value of abstinence, graphically depicted drinking as a virtual road to hell.

This early temperance work was often closely linked with religious organizations. Around 1800 churches began introducing abstinence pledges, in which congregants promised to abstain from liquor and sometimes to shun anyone else who drank. This credo was summed up by the title of a popular song of 1874, George T. Evans's "The Lips That Touch Liquor, Shall Never Touch Mine."

Many moderate politicians and citizens skeptically regarded people who refrained completely from drinking. They felt that rigid adherence to a "bone-dry" philosophy did more harm than good to the temperance movement, because it stifled individual freedom.

One such moderate was Abraham Lincoln, who famously remarked, "Prohibition will work great injury to the cause of temperance. It is a species of intemperance itself."[52]

Physical, Mental, Moral, and Social Concerns

Temperance advocates, both moderate and extreme, justified their position with many reasons. Some were primarily concerned with the moral or religious aspects of alcohol abuse. They considered drunkenness a failure of individual will and religious faith. Lyman Beecher, a prominent nineteenth-century minister, spoke for many when he said, "Intemperance is a national sin."[53]

Other people worried that excessive drinking was the cause of many physical and mental problems. Doctors recognized some of the obvious physical and mental effects of alcoholism, and some believed that drinking was the root of cancer and other diseases. A few zealots even made irrational claims that drunkards could catch fire if they got too close to a candle flame or could spontaneously combust.

"A Drink That Never Harms"

This verse is an educational lesson from a temperance pamphlet for children, published by the Women's Christian Temperance Union in the 1870s. It is reprinted in Edward Behr's Prohibition: Thirteen Years That Changed America.

"One, two, three, four, five fingers on every little hand. Listen while they speak to us; be sure we understand.

1 THERE IS A DRINK THAT NEVER HARMS It will make us strong.

2 THERE IS A DRINK THAT NEVER ALARMS Some drinks make people wicked.

3 A DRINK THAT KEEPS OUR SENSES RIGHT There are drinks that take away our senses.

4 A DRINK THAT MAKES OUR FACES BRIGHT We should never touch the drinks that will put evil into our hearts and spoil our faces.

5 GOD GIVES US THE ONLY DRINK—'TIS PURE, COLD WATER"

Some temperance advocates looked beyond the individual drinker and worried about the overall effect of drinking on society. Thomas R. Pegram writes, "Many nineteenth-century Americans believed passionately that drinking ruined lives and disrupted society. Over time, many more came to believe that the alcohol industry . . . directly and intentionally threatened the family, the social order, and democracy itself."[54]

Maine Leads the Nation

Although authorities were slow to legislate changes in the nation's drinking habits, laws did come. In 1831, for instance, the federal government did away with a daily liquor ration for soldiers. Progress on a national scale was slow, however, so temperance advocates had better legislative success at the state and local levels.

In this regard, Maine led the nation. In 1840 Portland, Maine, became the nation's first completely dry city, thanks largely to the efforts of one man: Neal Dow, a Quaker, tanner, and timber speculator. Dow became an increasingly influential man in Portland following his successful lobbying for a citywide dry law, and he was elected mayor in 1851.

As mayor, Dow zealously worked to clear his city of all liquor. His efforts included staging well-publicized saloon raids, in which gallons of illegal liquor were poured into street gutters. Such actions put him and his family in danger—they were victims of repeated muggings and vandalism—but he refused to back down or abandon his principles.

Dow's temperance philosophy spread rapidly across his state and the nation. In 1851, the same year Dow was elected mayor, Maine became the first state in America to pass a statewide dry law (which Dow had drafted). Other states soon followed, including Oregon, Minnesota, Rhode Island, Massachusetts, Vermont, and Michigan in 1852; Connecticut in 1854; and Iowa, Delaware, Pennsylvania, New York, and New Hampshire in 1855.

This flurry of activity faded, however, in the years before and during the Civil War. The nation's leaders and citizens were too preoccupied with the long war's devastation to worry about the country's drinking habits. In fact, overall drinking increased during the war years. Edward Behr notes, "The Civil War put a stop to the onward march of the Temperance movement—it was a time of excessive alcoholic indulgence."[55]

After the war, the movement resumed. A national political group, the Prohibition Party, was established in 1869 and in 1872 nominated its first presidential candidate, James Black. The keynote speaker at the party's national convention warned that alcohol was a great evil. Comparing alcohol to another, recently abolished practice, he stated, "Slavery is gone, but drunkenness stays."[56]

Female prohibitionists are depicted protesting outside a saloon. Women had always been allies to the temperance movement.

Women and Temperance

The Prohibition Party had no real impact on national politics, however, and only very limited success regionally. In fact, by the end of the nineteenth century it seemed that the temperance movement was beginning to lose momentum. Four dry states—Iowa, South Dakota, New Hampshire, and Vermont—actually went backward, repealing their dry laws and allowing the sale of liquor once again. Even Kansas, a longtime bastion of temperance, tolerated illegal saloons whose owners were willing to pay regular bribes to police and other authorities.

However, some groups vigorously continued to advance their anti-alcohol agendas. The most effective of these by far was a loose coalition of women's groups. Women had always been primary driving forces within the temperance movement. They frequently bore the brunt of the hardships that drunkenness caused within families, such as wages misspent in saloons and physical abuse from drunken husbands. Women were thus considered natural warriors in the fight against liquor.

The WCTU in Action

The largest and most effective of the women's organizations was the Women's Christian Temperance Union (WCTU). Founded in 1874 in Cleveland, Ohio, the organization soon had chapters in every state. Its membership came primarily from the middle class and, as the name suggests, typically had strong church ties.

The WCTU was not content simply to publish pamphlets or make speeches. It was an activist organization, and WCTU members conducted very public demonstrations and actions. Typical of these were marches in which groups of women and children entered male-only saloons, singing religious songs and praying loudly for the souls of present company. Clark writes that these women marched boldly in public, "offering themselves to the indignities of passive resistance, singing, praying, kneeling on sidewalks to suffer the sneers, curses, and often the manhandling of sometimes violently outraged men."[57]

Authorities sometimes arrested the protestors and often attempted to keep such embarrassing spectacles out of the public eye. However, WCTU members refused to be silent and made a point of openly defying authorities who tried to stop them. At the time, this "unladylike" behavior was considered a shocking display of aggression.

Fighting Back

WCTU demonstrators also used the media to their advantage. Through newspaper reports across the country, the public became increasingly aware of groups of women who deliberately broke laws and provoked police and politicians. In this way, the women drew attention to their cause.

The WCTU also conducted broader, politically oriented campaigns. In 1875, for instance, it petitioned Congress for national prohibition. This effort was unsuccessful, but the group fared better with smaller efforts, such as the introduction of courses on the evils of alcohol into the nation's public schools.

Saloon keepers and liquor manufacturers naturally opposed the WCTU, whose success would have put the liquor industry out of business. To counteract the WCTU's efforts, the liquor industry continued to push the message it had been promoting for years: Moderate alcohol consumption was benign and even healthy. One campaign by beer brewers, for instance, labeled beer (which is made with grain and yeast) a form of "liquid bread."

Other campaigns by the liquor industry sought to put full responsibility for alcohol abuse onto drinkers and their mothers and wives. One public message to the WCTU from a saloon association read: "Don't blame the saloonkeepers, ladies, BLAME THE UNGOVERNED AND UNGOVERNABLE BOYS YOU BRING UP."[58]

Frances Willard

Out of the many female temperance advocates of this era, two stood out. One was Frances Willard, the WCTU's first president. Willard was a deeply religious, devoted activist who once described the women's crusade against liquor as the "whirlwind of the Lord. . . . It has set forces in motion which each day become more potent, and will sweep on until the rum power in America is overthrown."[59]

Willard, the daughter of rigidly puritan Methodist parents, became a university professor before embarking on her career as a temperance organizer. She was a classic "bone-dry" prohibitionist who called

Prohibition advocate Frances Willard was a driving force in the prohibition movement.

even moderate drinking "the shoddy life-belt, which promises safety, but only tempts into danger, and fails in the hour of need . . . the fruitful fountain from which the flood of intemperance is fed."[60]

Carry Nation

Frances Willard was a formidable figure, but she was not nearly as fierce as America's most famous prohibitionist, Carry Nation. Edward Behr writes, "In the portrait gallery of Prohibition eccentrics, Carry Nation . . . stands out as the wildest, maddest, most frenzied crusader of all."[61]

Born Carry Moore in Kentucky in 1846, Nation survived poverty, her mother's mental instability, frequent ill health, an intermittent education, and her own mental illness. Despite these handicaps, she managed to earn a teaching certificate and in 1867 married a young physician, Charles Gloyd. She left him after a few months because of his alcoholism and in 1877 married David Nation, a lawyer, journalist, and minister. They settled in Kansas.

Smashing the Enemy

This passage is reprinted in Norman H. Clark's Deliver Us from Evil: An Interpretation of American Prohibition. *It describes a typical saloon raid by the fanatical antiliquor crusader, Carry Nation.*

"Mrs. Nation smashed one saloon's Venetian mirror with brickbats, flung stones through a second saloon's windows, leveled a half-brick at the head of a boy attempting to sweep up . . . ripped some candid and stimulating prints from the walls, powdered the bric-a-brac and glasses, separated the rungs from all chairs, drop-kicked a cuspidor [spittoon used for spitting out chewing tobacco] over a pot-bellied stove and threw a billiard ball at what she mistakenly took to be Satan lounging behind the bar. . . . Before leaving, she begged to be arrested and then sang a number of hymns, only to express herself as insulted when a saloon-keeper said it was the worst atrocity she had committed yet."

Carry Nation was an outspoken Prohibition activist who often brought a hatchet into saloons.

Nation had always disliked alcohol, but she did not become an activist until 1890, when a U.S. Supreme Court decision allowed the importation and sale of liquor from other states to Kansas. At that point, the voices she had long heard in her head began directing her to destroy the state's saloons.

Nation's method of dealing with saloons was simple and direct. Nearly six feet tall and always dressed in black, she entered saloons and smashed everything she saw with a hatchet or a hammer. All the while she sang, prayed, hurled insults and dire predictions, and lectured those unfortunate drinkers who happened to be there.

She was jailed and fined frequently for her "hatchetations." Newspaper photographers often portrayed her behind bars, reading her Bible and praying. Nation never stayed in jail long, though. No sheriff or mayor was eager to advertise the fact that the saloons she destroyed were illegal in the first place. Also, she was always able to pay her fines with income from lecture tours, sales of souvenir hatchets, and subscriptions to her newsletters, which had titles like the *Smasher's Mail*, the *Hatchet*, and the *Home Defender*.

Antiliquor crusades led by Nation and Frances Willard strongly influenced the Anti-Saloon League's efforts in later decades. It is doubtful that Prohibition could have happened without the decades of temperance work that preceded it.

Bootleggers and Gangsters: The Effects of Prohibition

All along, dry advocates had predicted that Prohibition could be cheaply enforced. When one 1920 report suggested that full enforcement would require the huge sum of $50 million annually, for instance, Wayne Wheeler countered that $5 million would do the job. Dry advocates also predicted that Prohibition enforcement would be simple and easy. They assumed that most Americans would respect any law of the land, even if they disapproved of or resented that law. This was undoubtedly true for millions.

When it came to millions more, however, the hopeful predictions and assumptions proved naïve. The first reported violation of the Volstead Act took place within an hour of the official start of Prohibition. Early on the morning of January 17, 1920, six armed men in Chicago stole one hundred thousand dollars worth of whiskey stockpiled for legal medicinal use.

This robbery was just the beginning. America, it turned out, was full of people who wanted to drink, and criminals who were happy to help them do so. Edward Behr writes that the men who wrote the Volstead Act grossly underestimated "the willingness of the lawbreakers to risk conviction, the degree of human ingenuity displayed to get around [the act's] provisions, and the ease with which the lawbreakers would be able to subvert all those whose job was to enforce it."[62]

Legal Challenges

Across America, local authorities had various reactions to the new law. Most states enacted their own laws that supported the national measure. Other state leaders, however, openly opposed it. Connecticut and Rhode Island, for instance, never ratified the Eighteenth Amendment and provided minimal local help to federal enforcement agents. Maryland officials also consistently refused to cooperate with Prohibition, and New Jersey governor Edward I. Edwards, an avowed wet, declared his hope that the state he led would remain "as wet as the Atlantic Ocean."[63]

Some state leaders even passed laws that directly contradicted the national legislation. The legislatures of New York, New Jersey, and Massachusetts, for instance, passed laws in 1920 that allowed the production and sale of beer and wine higher in alcoholic content than the

0.5 percent national limit. Such measures were short-lived, however. Later that year, the Supreme Court rejected as unconstitutional all state laws that violated the national law.

The Supreme Court also rejected several other legal challenges to Prohibition, made on the grounds that Prohibition itself was not constitutional. One came from Elihu Root, a cabinet-level statesman under Presidents William McKinley and Theodore Roosevelt, who was now a lawyer representing a New Jersey brewer. Root argued that the Eighteenth Amendment was unconstitutional, violated the enforcement powers of individual states, and stifled the right of local self-government. His efforts were futile, however. Root lost his case.

Loopholes

Once the Supreme Court decided that Prohibition was constitutional, people began to look for ways to get around it. The Volstead Act had plenty of loopholes; that is, there were explicit exemptions within the law that allowed alcohol production and consumption by certain groups. It did not take enterprising producers, drinkers, and bootleggers long to simply define themselves as members of these groups. One exemption, for instance, allowed American distilleries to produce whiskey if it was bound overseas for nonbeverage, medicinal

Alcohol raids were common during Prohibition. Many Americans tried to take advantage of loopholes in the prohibition law.

"Quite Frank Disregard"

A presidential panel on crime control, the Wickersham Commission, offered considerable evidence in 1931 that Prohibition was being flagrantly violated. This passage from its report is reprinted in Henry Lee's book How Dry We Were: Prohibition Revisited.

"There is a mass of evidence before us as to a general prevalence of drinking in homes, in clubs, and in hotels, of drinking parties given and attended by persons of high standing and respectability; of drinking by tourists at winter and summer resorts; and of drinking in connection with public dinners and at conventions. . . . It is evident that, taking the country as a whole, people of wealth, business men and professional men, and their families, and perhaps the higher paid workingmen, and their families, are drinking in large numbers in quite frank disregard of the National Prohibition Act."

uses such as the production of cough syrup. Hundreds of thousands of gallons of alcohol were distilled for this market but never reached offshore destinations. Presumably, it found its way to drinkers in America.

Another loophole involved doctors who prescribed alcohol for medical purposes (such as for treatment programs that gradually detoxified alcoholics). After 1920 authorities noted huge increases in doctor-prescribed, 95 percent pure alcohol. In Chicago alone, immediately after Prohibition began, more than fifteen thousand doctors and fifty-seven thousand retail druggists applied for licenses to prescribe or sell medicinal alcohol. These doctors, many of whom could be persuaded to write bogus prescriptions, helped drive up nationwide sales of medicinal alcohol 400 percent between 1923 and 1931. One prescription written by a Detroit doctor read, "Take three ounces every hour for stimulant until stimulated."[64]

Yet another loophole concerned low-alcohol "near-beer." This was still legal; however, the only way to brew it was to make full-strength beer and then remove the alcohol. Unscrupulous brewers, writer Frederick Lewis Allen notes, found it "excessively easy to fail to remove [the excess alcohol] from the entire product."[65]

Sacramental Wine

Wine for religious functions was still legal as well. Practicing Jewish families, for instance, were allowed one gallon per adult member per year. The approved wine was rationed according to the number of registered worshipers in synagogues. Roman Catholic churches were similarly regulated.

It has been estimated that the demand for sacramental wine increased by eight hundred thousand gallons during the first two years of Prohibition. Authorities suggested, however, that not all of this wine was used for genuine religious services. As a spokesman for the Federal Council of the Churches of Christ in America put it, "Not more than one-quarter of this is sacramental—the rest is sacrilegious."[66]

Some of the demand for sacramental wine was out-and-out fraud. One six-hundred-member "synagogue" turned out to be a laundry. In another case, a thousand gallons of wine was given to a synagogue that turned out to be nothing more than a postal address in a tenement building. And an organization called the Assembly of Hebrew Orthodox Rabbis of America, on investigation, was revealed to consist of one person—an Irishman named Sullivan.

Home Brewing

Home brewers, meanwhile, could legally manufacture nonintoxicating cider and juices for personal consumption. However, some juices, especially grape juice, can easily be fermented into wine. All home brewers had to do was leave the grape juice unrefrigerated so that the yeast that naturally clings to the grapes could help the sugar in them ferment into alcohol.

Thus, the compacted blocks, or bricks, of California raisins used to make grape juice became extremely popular with home brewers. Distributors carefully warned buyers not to combine the brick with water and set it aside, because then the juice would ferment. Despite this warning, or perhaps because of it, mail-order business for the bricks was so popular that California's grape production increased tenfold between 1920 and 1933.

Home brewers produced many other kinds of alcohol as well. For instance, the makings for a potent form of gin called "bathtub gin" could be legally bought from pharmacies. The basic ingredients for home-brewed beer—malt, barley, and yeast—were even easier to find.

Meanwhile, thousands of small home stills for making illegal whiskey (often called "moonshine" or, more vividly, "rotgut") appeared in both rural and urban locales. Corn sugar, essential to the brewing of corn whiskey, was easy to find, and its production increased sixfold between 1919 and 1929. One Prohibition Bureau official estimated that by the end of the 1920s home stills provided the largest percentage of the illegal liquor in the country—seven to eight times more than was being smuggled in or diverted from legal sources.

Policemen often had to confiscate distilling equipment like this. People manufactured liquor in their homes with such apparatuses.

Bootleggers

However, not even the widespread creation and distribution of home brew, medicinal alcohol, and sacramental wine could satisfy the nation's thirst for illegal liquor. People wanted more. As a result, all across the country gangs of criminals turned to bootlegging—that is, smuggling and distributing illegal alcohol.

Many observers have noted that Prohibition gave rise to organized crime in America by creating an atmosphere in which criminal gangs, which until then had been loosely organized and small in scale, could grow into large, organized crime networks. Thanks to the enormous amounts of money made from bootlegging, the small gangs were able to thrive and expand.

Criminals quickly learned that the public was willing to pay inflated prices for liquor, and bootlegging made many small-time thugs into millionaires. Just twenty months into Prohibition, the Internal Revenue Bureau estimated that bootlegging was a billion-dollar business. The tax agency further estimated that $32 million in uncollected federal alcohol taxes were being lost every year.

This money allowed underworld gangs to invest in new technologies that boosted their criminal activities. For instance, better weapons, first developed in wartime, helped the bootleggers defend themselves against rivals as well as government agents. Faster cars and boats helped them get their product past the authorities. Sometimes, however, bootleggers did not even need to avoid the authorities. Another factor aiding the gangs was the ease with which some policemen and other enforcement agents could be bribed to ignore smuggling operations.

Al Capone

Violence in this atmosphere was almost inevitable, as gangs fought to gain and control territory or operations. Gang rivalry created frequent and bloody confrontations, and Prohibition became the backdrop for untold numbers of violent stories. The most famous of the Prohibition-era hoodlums was Al "Scarface" Capone. Norman H. Clark notes that Capone's career revealed "how the Prohibition laws shaped an environment of greed, envy, cynicism, fear, carnal sin, corruption, and mass murder."[67]

Capone's territory was Chicago, one of the cities where gang violence was most flagrant. He was responsible for, or was the target of, dozens of gang-related attacks and bloody turf wars. The best known of these was the 1929 St. Valentine's Day Massacre, in which members of Capone's gang gunned down seven members of George "Bugs" Moran's rival gang.

Bodies of murdered gangsters lie in a Chicago warehouse after the St. Valentine's Day Massacre between the gangs of Al Capone and George "Bugs" Moran.

"Joe Sent Me"

The main outlets for liquor provided by gangsters were illegal, unmarked clubs called speakeasies, or speaks. Many speakeasies were simply renovated saloons. With a little modification, the main rooms of the saloons became perfectly legal (if uncrowded) restaurants; their covert drinking areas were behind doors, typically in former kitchens. Other speakeasies were concealed behind anonymous doors in basements, office buildings, and garages. Typically, they admitted only members or those with recommendations; "Joe sent me" became a cliché of the era, typifying how the secretive nature of these recommendations hid speakeasies from the police.

Speaks multiplied quickly across the country. By 1925 New York City alone had about thirty thousand, twice as many as the city's pre-Prohibition bars, restaurants, and nightclubs put together. By 1927 that number had risen to one hundred thousand. In fact, there were so many speaks on a single Manhattan boulevard—East 52nd Street—that homeowners were forced to put signs in their windows: "This is a private residence. Do not ring."[68] In general, liquor was everywhere; in some ways, it was as easy to drink during Prohibition as before it. Humorist Will Rogers commented, "Prohibition is better than no liquor at all."[69]

The style of speakeasies varied widely. Some were dark, dank places populated by somber alcoholics and prostitutes. Others were elaborate establishments with lavish decorations offering the best in live music and entertainment. Jazz greats Louis Armstrong and Duke Ellington were only two of the thousands of musicians whose careers were boosted by the Prohibition-era demand for live performance to go along with food and drink.

Alcohol and Crime

Although speakeasies began appearing in the early months of Prohibition, it seemed at first that the new law was working reasonably well. The overall crime rate fell. The country's overall liquor consumption dropped. Drinking among the working class fell steeply, since speakeasies charged more for liquor than the average blue-collar worker could afford regularly. The medical news was also good. Deaths from cirrhosis of the liver and other alcohol-related problems declined significantly. The editor-owner of the *Seattle Times*, who had once opposed Prohibition, commented that his mind had changed as a result of such reports. He wrote, "It makes me sorry we did not have Prohibition long ago. Yes, sir, we have found in Seattle that it is better to buy shoes than booze."[70]

Speakeasies, like the one depicted here, were illegal saloons often run by gangsters. Passwords were necessary to get into the establishments.

However, the early results were misleading. After a brief initial drop in the overall crime rate, the only crimes that continued to decline were minor ones such as swearing, vandalism, and vagrancy. Serious crime was another matter, as the ruthless bootlegging trade encouraged felonies such as theft and homicide.

In fact, the overall crime rate in America skyrocketed during the 1920s. The rates for serious crimes (such as murder, burglary, and assault) increased by nearly 13 percent. The murder rate rose alarmingly; in the cities, homicides jumped from 5.6 per 100,000 before Prohibition to nearly 10 per 100,000 during the era. Arrests for public drunkenness, drunk driving, and disorderly conduct also rose steeply.

Many observers of the time, looking at such statistics, believed that Prohibition was making life worse than it had been before the law took effect. After visiting the United States, the English essayist G.K. Chesterton remarked, "Alcoholism has never threatened disaster as it is threatening America today."[71]

Liver Disease

Skyrocketing crime was not the only dangerous result of Prohibition. The statistics for drinking-related disease and death also rose sharply after an initial decline. Although cases of the deadly disease cirrhosis of the liver had dropped in the first years of the century, they rose steadily during the 1920s, a clear indication of heavier drinking. Some observers argue that this was because both suppliers and drinkers were attracted to higher-potency hard liquor such as whiskey. Hard liquor was easier to transport and to store than beer or wine, and it offered a bigger, faster kick.

Other researchers speculate that cirrhosis rates increased because the uncertainty of liquor supplies tended to make people drink to excess. One newspaperman recalled, "Everybody drank as though there would never be another drink. If you opened a bottle, you killed it."[72]

Bad Liquor

Another cause of death and injury was the drinking of industrial, or denatured, alcohol. This was a form of alcohol, used for a variety of purposes in the chemical industry, that was still legal during Prohibition. Some unscrupulous bootleggers made their liquor using denatured alcohol or commercial products that contained it, such as embalming fluid, antifreeze solution, and rubbing alcohol.

Denatured alcohol is highly poisonous, and drinking it can result in death, blindness, or paralysis. The results of its use in bootleg whiskey during Prohibition were horrifying. There are no accurate records, but one study reported that deaths in America from liquor made with industrial alcohol rose from 1,064 in 1920 to 4,154 in 1925. It has been estimated that by 1927 the figures may have quadrupled, with hundreds of thousands more blinded or paralyzed through alcohol poisoning. In the single year 1930, in one county in Kansas, there were 15,000 victims of alcohol poisoning. In the early 1930s, some 50,000 people were permanently paralyzed after drinking a poisonous concoction from Jamaica called "jake."

The Bureau Tries

In the face of these frightening statistics, authorities found it was impossible to make more than a dent in enforcing Prohibition. The sheer volume of bootlegging alone, much less the rise in related crimes, overwhelmed them. Prohibition Bureau head Lincoln Andrews, who took charge of the agency in 1925, later estimated that during Prohibition government agents found only about 5 percent of all the liquor smuggled into the country.

One reason was simply the small number of agents on hand. The Prohibition Bureau was authorized to hire, at most, only about three

Club patrons buy drinks from a bar during Prohibition. The government tried to control bootlegging but uncovered only a small percentage of the illegal operations.

thousand agents at any given time. This small force, divided into district offices, had to cover nearly nineteen thousand miles of coastline, find and destroy hundreds of thousands of well-hidden, well-guarded stills and speakeasies, and carry out many other tasks as well. One historian calculated that if the entire army of agents had been arrayed along America's borders and coastlines, there would have been only one man to patrol every twelve miles and no one left to look after the country's interior, much less supervise the manufacture of legal alcohol.

Another reason agents had such trouble was that the Prohibition Bureau received little support from other agencies. The Coast Guard and Customs Service helped a little, but they did not have enough manpower to supply personnel on a regular basis. In addition, rivalries and disagreements among agencies often slowed the bureau's efforts.

Making the bureau's job still more difficult was the fact that Canada, which had its own prohibition laws, repealed these laws in the early 1920s. Once alcohol became legal again north of the border, Canadian distilleries and breweries became rich supply sources for American bootleggers, who easily penetrated the long border between the countries.

Although many smugglers operated across the border by land, and a very few by airplane, smuggling by boat was the easiest and most reliable method. Many legitimate fishermen turned to the business, since it was relatively easy work that paid much better than fishing. One Massachusetts fisherman recalled, "You knew right away when a man stopped fishing and started running rum. In the first place, his family began to eat proper and you could tell by what they bought at the grocery store, when [before] they had had to run up a grub bill [credit] all winter."[73]

Political Jobs

Political maneuvering, in the nation's capital and elsewhere, also severely constrained the bureau. One example of this was the decision not to make Prohibition agents civil service employees. The decision exempted agents from civil service rules, which set minimum standards for background checks, job training, and ethical standards. There were, in effect, no prerequisites, background checks, or training programs for agents. All that anyone needed to become an agent was the endorsement of the ASL or a prominent politician. As a result, thousands of Prohibition agents were incompetent and inexperienced. Some even had prior criminal records.

The ASL and other backers of the Volstead Act justified this decision by claiming that the act would not have been approved if bureau agents had been required to become civil service employees. A more

Under the Noses of the Police

One of the most flagrant examples of illegal liquor manufacture, operating openly in the presence of police and other authorities, was that of the Genna brothers, who for several years were Chicago's most prolific bootleggers. In this passage from Prohibition, *Edward Behr describes the Genna operation:*

"Although their criminal record was a long one, they had obtained a license to make large quantities of industrial alcohol, farming the job out to slum-based Sicilian families using primitive home stills, who delivered the liquor to a Genna-owned warehouse factory within four blocks of the Maxwell Street police station, one of the largest in town.

Here the raw alcohol was turned into whiskey and gin—40,000 quarts of alcohol at about 50 cents a quart producing 120,000 quarts of bootleg 'ersatz' whiskey and gin costing anything from $15 to $60 a bottle. No attempt was made at concealment. In any case, the factory ingredients—creosote, iodine, burnt sugar, fusel oil, cane sugar, oil of juniper—gave off considerable telltale odors, which only the Maxwell Street policemen seemed unable to detect.

A former manager later told investigators the factory operated on shifts, twenty-four hours a day, with heavy trucks constantly parked outside:

The warehouse was run openly and in full view of everybody, unmolested [undisturbed] by the State authorities other than an occasional raid. But notification of 24 hours was always given to the Gennas. Sometimes the very letters sent out by the police ordering the raid were shown to them. There would be a clean-up, then a raid, then a re-opening. During all the period that I worked there the entire Genna enterprise was done with the full knowledge, consent and approval of the Chicago police.'"

stringent code for Prohibition agents, they argued, would not have found favor with enough state lawmakers to have been voted into law.

As a result of the exemption, unscrupulous political appointments were commonplace. A job as a Prohibition agent became, in many cases, little more than a reward for loyalty to an officeholder. Edward Behr comments that, in every state, recruitment was "an integral part of the spoils system, in the hands of local politicians whose careers depended on patronage."[74]

Corruption

The maximum salary for an agent, $2,300 a year, was barely enough to live on; New York City garbage collectors earned more. Nonetheless, being a Prohibition agent was considered an excellent position because it offered the potential to earn extra (if illegal) money. The temptation was strong, and the opportunities plentiful, to accept bribes, steal confiscated goods, issue illegal permits, or extort protection money. In any given year, roughly ten thousand people applied for two thousand open jobs.

Certainly not all agents were corrupt. Many did resist, choosing to live on their low salaries. The most famous example is Elliott Ness. This Chicago-based agent led a team of agents known as the Untouchables, so called because they were resistant to bribery.

A large portion of agents, however, did succumb to bribery, and most of those who did lived lavishly. They ate expensive meals, bought fancy cars or homes, gambled, and otherwise flaunted their sudden wealth. Behr comments, "The discrepancy between Prohibition agents' low salaries and their life-styles was staggering—some of them even showing up for work in chauffeur-driven cars."[75]

Even legitimate "sting" operations were opportunities for corrupt agents to pad their expense accounts. One effort to shut down New York's speakeasies, for instance, resulted in $8,400 in fines for violators—but also in $75,000 in bar bills, paid for by the government.

Graft

Such corruption was widespread. Between 1920 and 1926, one out of every twelve bureau agents was fired for graft (violations of the job). One Detroit regional director recalled interviewing about three thousand applicants and hiring eighty; after one month, sixty of them had been fired. "It was a great mess," he recalled. "Sometimes an agent would go to work on Monday and on Wednesday or Thursday would be grafting."[76]

The problem of graft was not limited to bureau agents. Many others in government were susceptible. Mabel Willebrand, deputy attorney general in charge of Prohibition enforcement, charged in 1928, "The influence of liquor in politics begins down in the City wards and often in county districts, *but it extends if it can up to the Cabinet and the White House in Washington.*"[77]

Corruption was particularly common among local police forces. Many officers could be persuaded to look the other way, or even pitch in, during smuggling operations. One rum runner recalled, "I have seen policemen take off their caps and coats, assist bootleggers in unloading and then sit down and enjoy a drinking party."[78]

A man reads a sign directing the way to a speakeasy. Such establishments were widespread and continued operating by bribing police and government officials with alcohol and money.

Believing in Santa

In 1927 an attempt was made to change the situation by altering the law. Congress amended the Volstead Act so that the bureau came under the jurisdiction of the Justice Department. Also, bureau agents finally became subject to civil service regulations. Even after this attempt to reform the bureau, however, corruption remained rampant. The temptation to pick up easy money, free liquor, or other illegal rewards was simply too strong. Frederick Lewis Allen comments:

Izzy and Moe

Some Prohibition agents could not carry out their duties; they were corrupt, or hampered by political or other constraints. Many others, however, were successful. History's most well known were Elliott Ness and his group of agents, the Untouchables. During Prohibition, however, the most famous agents in America were Izzy Einstein and his partner, Moe Smith.

Physically, the two were not made for working incognito—Einstein was five feet tall and weighed 225 pounds, and Smith was even more obese. Despite their distinctive appearances, however, the two excelled at undercover work.

Their methods were as unusual as their looks. Einstein was a ham who loved to use disguises and fake accents. To trick bootleggers and speakeasy owners, he plausibly impersonated such characters as a socialite, a judge in a beauty contest, and a Southern colonel. Unaware they were dealing with a government agent, the liquor dealers sold their goods to Einstein and he arrested them.

The pair's work took them to various cities, but their base was New York. Together, Einstein and Smith accounted for 20 percent of all Prohibition arrests in Manhattan between 1920 and 1925. They often made twenty to thirty arrests a week, and once raided seventeen places in one night, even though their names and faces were familiar to millions of newspaper readers across the country.

Anybody who believed that men employable at thirty-five or forty or fifty dollars a week would surely have the expert technical knowledge and the diligence to supervise successfully the complicated chemical operations of industrial-alcohol plants or to outwit the craftiest devices of smugglers and bootleggers, and that they would surely have the force of character to resist corruption by men whose pockets were bulging with money, would be ready to believe also in Santa Claus, perpetual motion, and pixies.[79]

A Neglected Law

Prohibition might have been more effective, many historians argue, if the government had committed enough resources to support it. However, this support never came. Pegram comments, "American government, at all levels, failed that test."[80]

Instead, Prohibition suffered from neglect. Once it was passed, the law was allowed to languish with a bare minimum of maintenance. The bureau never received enough resources to do its job. Neither President Harding nor his successor, Calvin Coolidge, asked for greater power to enforce Prohibition. Congress, for its part, passed only a few small amendments to the Volstead Act, including increased sentences for violators and legislation that banned doctors from prescribing beer.

It appeared that lawmakers were simply prepared to ignore Prohibition. Their speeches emphasized the moral duty of Americans to obey the rules, but otherwise politicians generally avoided open support of the law. This was, in large part, because they were hesitant to risk alienating the many voters who hated Prohibition. Frederick Lewis Allen notes that Congress was "unwilling to face the music; there was a comfortable dry majority in both Houses, but it was one thing to be a dry and quite another to insist on enforcement at whatever cost and whatever inconvenience to some of one's influential constituents."[81]

The System Begins to Collapse

Meanwhile, there was precious little money to enforce Prohibition on the state level. By 1927 many states provided no funds at all for enforcement. The total expenditures for Prohibition enforcement by the states equaled one-fourth of what they spent to maintain parks and monuments, and one-eighth of the amount spent on enforcing fish and game laws.

This lack of funding led to sharp decreases in the bureau's ability to arrest and prosecute violators. As the 1920s wore on, efforts to enforce Prohibition grew increasingly haphazard. In some areas of the country, wrongdoers were zealously prosecuted. In others, they were virtually ignored.

Some states addressed the problem by simply repealing their individual enforcement acts. This, in essence, absolved them of any responsibility for prosecuting wrongdoers. New York was the first to do so in 1923, followed by Massachusetts, Montana, and Wisconsin. Cities that were tolerant of drinking increasingly witnessed court cases decided by jurors who nullified the law; many juries simply refused to convict even defendants who were clearly guilty of violations.

Even states that conscientiously upheld the law had problems. For example, their courts were inundated with so many arrests that their already overworked judicial systems came close to collapse. Without the funds to hire more clerks and judges, many courts held "bargain days," when Prohibition offenders who waived jury trials and pled guilty received only small fines or probation.

Not Working

Anti-Saloon League chapters in each state, as well as the league's main office in the nation's capital, demanded better enforcement. These calls, however, were ignored. The ASL could not convince enough politicians to pass tighter legislation. In part this was because the league no longer enjoyed the power it once had. The organization's base of support among voters had begun to erode shortly after Prohibition became law. Many league supporters, assuming their work was done, had stopped contributing money or writing letters to their lawmakers. As early as 1921, the director of the ASL's New York chapter, William Anderson, alluded to the crumbling structure of the organization when he bluntly announced, "The Anti-Saloon League is afflicted with dry rot."[82]

More problems followed in the next few years. Anderson himself was convicted of altering the league's accounting books to cover expenses. Then, as the result of an investigation by the Federal Council of Churches criticizing the league's political strategy, the league lost the support of the nation's organized churches. A final blow came in 1927 with the death of Wayne Wheeler.

The ASL was losing much of its power and relevance. It was clear that Prohibition was not working, and millions of Americans were openly contemptuous of the law. Writer and editor H.L. Mencken commented, "The business of evading Prohibition and making mock of it has ceased to wear any aspects of crime, and has become a sort of national sport."[83] The stage was set: The Eighteenth Amendment was about to become the only constitutional amendment in American history to be repealed.

CHAPTER 5

Drinking Again: Repeal and the Lessons of Prohibition

Even when Prohibition was relatively young, its weaknesses were obvious. The law was impossible to enforce, and corruption and political concerns hobbled the Prohibition Bureau. Throughout the 1920s, meanwhile, defiance of the law became increasingly open. *Time* magazine printed a recipe for gin. The wife of the Speaker of the House of Representatives admitted that she kept a small still in her house. And Fiorello LaGuardia, the colorful New York congressman (and future mayor of New York City), demonstrated at a press conference how to make beer.

Such incidents represented a growing sympathy for repeal. While many considered Prohibition simply a nuisance, for others it represented much more. To many opponents the law threatened the basic American principle of individual rights. They worried that, if Prohibition remained, the likelihood increased that other individual liberties could be taken away as well. Writer Michael Monahan noted this concern in 1920 when he stated, "To believe that Prohibition will stand is, in my view, to believe that the Republic [the United States] has lost her way and is without the guiding light of her noblest traditions."[84]

However, it did not seem that Prohibition could easily be repealed. Many Americans, both wet and dry, believed that—for better or worse—a constitutional amendment, once ratified, was set in stone. Clarence Darrow, the famous defense attorney and an avowed wet, stated in 1924: "Even to modify the Volstead Act would require a political revolution. To repeal the Eighteenth Amendment is well-nigh inconceivable."[85] For his part, Senator Morris Sheppard, still a passionate dry spokesman, proclaimed, "There is as much a chance of repealing the Eighteenth Amendment as there is for a hummingbird to fly to Mars with the Washington Monument tied to its tail."[86]

The AAPA

Despite such conviction, the political forces in favor of repeal were gathering strength. A number of activist groups formed, composed of middle-class professionals with no connections with the liquor industry. This gave the groups great credibility, since they had no financial interest in dispensing with Prohibition.

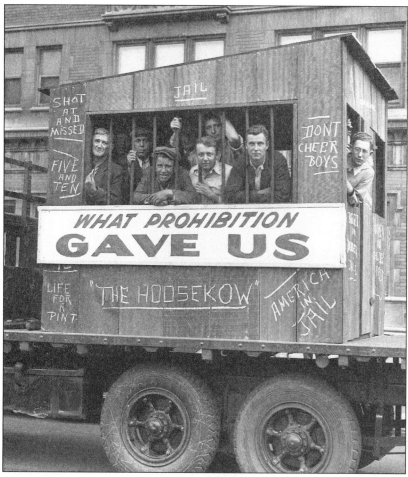

*A parade display lobbies for repeal of prohibition. Many felt Prohibition was
a governmental intrusion on personal privacy.*

The largest and most influential of these groups was the Association
Against the Prohibition Amendment (AAPA). This organization boasted
among its members a number of prominent business leaders, including
industrialist Pierre S. du Pont and banker Charles H. Sabin. Founded in 1918
and active throughout the 1920s, the AAPA, more than any other single
group, shaped the end of Prohibition.

The organization's position was that Prohibition was an illegal intrusion of the federal government into business as well as private affairs. It argued that repeal would benefit businesses, since legal liquor
could be taxed and business taxes could then be lowered. The AAPA
also supported repeal because the group favored states' rights and
thought Prohibition violated those rights. One member asserted, "The
Prohibition Amendment is not merely an impairment of the principle

of self-government of the States, *it constitutes an absolute abandon-ment of that principle.*"[57]

Women for Repeal

A number of other prominent groups were also voicing their support for repeal. Among these were lawyers' groups, state bar associations, and the American Bar Association. The American Federation of Labor, the union representing a majority of the nation's factory workers, gave its support to repeal. Meanwhile, the American Legion, repre-senting millions of World War I veterans, likewise urged an end to Prohibition.

Among the most powerful voices were women's groups. This seemed somewhat contradictory, since women had played such an important role in the early antialcohol movement. In fact, supporters of both Pro-hibition and repeal had expected that women's groups would continue to be overwhelmingly pro-dry.

However, the times were changing and millions of women now supported repeal. In part, this was a reflection of women's changing roles in society. They could vote now, and they were also increasingly important members of the workforce. Furthermore, women could openly drink; during Prohibition, it became acceptable (if still slightly scandalous) for speakeasies to include women, unlike the men-only saloons of pre-Prohibition days.

The Jazz Age

Women were not the only segment of American society that sup-ported repeal. The younger generation as a whole was also over-whelmingly in favor of it. For them, self-indulgence and personal freedom was all-important. This indulgence included such pleasures as drinking, sexual experimentation, and carefree entertainment, so much so that the 1920s was nicknamed the Jazz Age.

In part, this mood was a response to the deprivation, death, and uncertainty of World War I. More than a hundred thousand Ameri-can soldiers had died during that conflict, and twice that number had been wounded. The war also consumed a significant part of the coun-try's financial resources—about 20 percent at its peak—and rebuild-ing Europe afterward required further millions of dollars in American loans and humanitarian aid.

Americans thus had made serious sacrifices during and just after the war. They had done without items that were rationed for the war effort and, in many cases, had withstood the loss of family members. Now, remembering the war and their years of sacrifice, Americans, especially young people, were eager to enjoy themselves. Frederick Lewis Allen writes: "A whole generation had been infected by the eat-drink-and-be-merry-for-tomorrow-we-die spirit which accompanied the departure of the soldiers to the training camps and the fighting front."[88]

With this live-for-today attitude, illegal drinking became socially acceptable, even encouraged, among young people during the 1920s. Polls indicated that two out of three college students drank during Prohibition, a sharp increase over previous decades.

The 1928 Elections

As popular opinion in favor of repeal gained strength, the issue continued to be hotly debated. It was a pivotal issue in the 1928 presidential election. Al Smith, the governor of New York and a repeal supporter, received that year's Democratic nomination. About half of Smith's telegram formally accepting the nomination concerned Prohibition, an indication of how important the topic was in the election. Whoever won, Smith stated, would have to deal with a situation "entirely unsatisfactory to the great mass of our people." He stopped short of advocating outright repeal, however, which he felt was too large a step for the nation as a whole to take. He urged instead a less radical move: making Prohibition subject only to local-option laws and the "democratic principles of local self-government and states' rights."[89]

Despite Smith's position and the growing support of repeal, the 1928 elections were a victory for dry forces. The largest percentage in history of acknowledged drys was elected or returned to Congress. Furthermore, the antirepeal Republican candidate for president, Herbert Hoover, beat Smith in a landslide victory. Although this result seems odd in light of support for repeal, some observers feel that the election went that way because voters hoped to maintain the illusion that Prohibition, to them a symbol of solid family values, was still viable. Behr asserts, "The myth of a God-fearing, prosperous, hardworking dry America was more attractive to a majority of voters than Al Smith's realistic, more tolerant approach."[90]

The Depression Begins

As president, Hoover honored his commitment to uphold Prohibition, which he called "a great social and economic experiment, noble in motive and far-reaching in purpose."[91] He authorized tougher fines and jail terms for lawbreakers as well as the construction of more federal prisons to house Volstead violators. However, Hoover's efforts to uphold Prohibition did nothing to prevent a disaster that struck less than a year into his term of office. In October 1929 the stock market crashed. Suddenly the investments that businesses and individual

Two women dance on the roof of a Chicago hotel. Women became some of the most ardent supporters of repeal.

Americans had made during the 1920s were worthless. Widespread economic panic followed, and the country was plunged into the Great Depression. All across America, factories and stores closed, banks failed, and millions were hungry and unemployed. At one point, one hundred thousand people per week lost their jobs.

Economists, business leaders, and politicians searched desperately for ways to change the situation. One option was to reconsider repeal in economic terms. With Prohibition, the government lost millions of dollars yearly in potential taxes on liquor. During the affluent 1920s, there had been plenty of spare cash in circulation and these lost revenues had not been a major concern. Repeal advocates argued that they could be replaced by reinstating a tax on legal liquor.

Businessmen for Repeal

For many business leaders, an interest in repeal was not based on moral, religious, or altruistic grounds. Legalized and taxable alcohol was simply good business, because it represented the possibility of lower business taxes. The income the government received from business taxes could be replaced by income from liquor taxes.

This reflected another changing attitude. Before the Great Depression, industrialists had generally favored Prohibition because it meant increased profits for their businesses. Norman H. Clark notes of that earlier time, "Paychecks formerly pumped into the saloons were being converted into radios, automobiles, movie tickets, food, clothing, and real estate; neither the bootleggers nor the speakeasies presented any serious threat to the efficiency of industrial production."[92]

Now, however, businessmen were seeing things differently. They were losing money because Americans could not afford to buy their products. Their profits were falling but their taxes remained high. Thus, many businessmen hoped that a liquor tax could lessen or even completely eliminate the need for income and business taxes. Pierre S. du

Ford on Drinking

Automobile mogul Henry Ford remained a staunch supporter of Prohibition even as repeal seemed certain. His reasons for continuing to support the cause are reprinted in Edward Behr's Prohibition: Thirteen Years That Changed America:

"For myself, if booze ever comes back to the U.S. I am through with manufacturing. . . . I wouldn't be interested in putting autos into the hands of a generation soggy with drink.

With booze in control we can count on only two or three effective days work a week in the factory—and that would destroy the short day and the five-day week which sober industry has introduced. When men were drunk two or three days a week, industry had to have a ten- or twelve-hour day and a seven-day week.

With sobriety the working man can have an eight-hour day and a five-day week with the same or greater pay. . . . I would not be able to build a car that will run 200,000 miles if booze were around, because I wouldn't have accurate workmen."

A truck gathers petitions to support a modification of the Volstead Act. Many businessmen wanted a repeal to help boost business and lower taxes.

Pont, for example, grandly claimed that a tax on liquor "would be sufficient to pay off the entire debt of the United States . . . in a little less than fifteen years."[93]

Business leaders further predicted that repeal would be a cure-all for a wide range of problems. Repeal would do more than improve the overall economy, they said; it would also lower crime rates and create a more just government because local jurisdictions could make their own decisions about liquor. Interestingly, these predictions were similar to those that Prohibition supporters had made a decade earlier. Historian Larry Engelmann comments:

> After 1929, wet spokesmen argued not only that their measure would bring law and order, a restoration of the proper distribution of power between the federal government and local governments, and true temperance, but also an end to the depression, the undermining of radical movements that had sprung up among the unemployed, and a new industrial Eden as perfect as that promised years earlier by the prohibitionists.[94]

Hoover Loses Support

Business leaders were not the only ones who were increasingly supporting repeal. Newspaper polls from 1927 on had been revealing growing prorepeal majorities among voters. Meanwhile, the president's

71

actions were turning those voters against him. Hoover's reaction to the Great Depression, and to the nation's very real misery, was aloof and hands-off. As people continued to lose their jobs and families went hungry, citizens refused to believe his assurances that the country was on the verge of prosperity again.

Furthermore, his insistence on continuing to support Prohibition seemed increasingly irrelevant. Compared with the country's urgent need for relief, Hoover's continued insistence on upholding Prohibition at all costs appeared trivial and foolish. Pegram comments, "The depression made Hoover's resolution to enforce prohibition seem desperately misplaced."[95]

President Franklin D. Roosevelt was elected partly because he supported repeal. Soon after his presidency began he nullified the Eighteenth Amendment.

Although the president seemed uninterested, the nation's overall support of repeal was reflected in the actions of Congress. In March 1932, a House vote on repealing the Eighteenth Amendment was held. It failed, but just barely. The closeness of the vote indicated that congressional support was strong and the idea of repeal was workable. Meanwhile, as the 1932 presidential elections neared, repeal and the nation's economic crisis proved to be major factors in Hoover's failure to be reelected.

Enter Roosevelt

That year, the front-runner for the Democratic nomination for president was Franklin Delano Roosevelt, the charismatic governor of New York. Roosevelt personally favored repeal. However, he was cautious about publicly committing himself and the Democratic Party to the cause until he was satisfied that public opinion overwhelmingly supported it.

That satisfaction came once Roosevelt learned about several reports indicating that a majority of Americans—and Democrats—favored repeal. The most influential of these was a poll conducted by the *Literary Digest* magazine, which projected that three-quarters of Americans favored repeal. These figures included majorities in all states but Kansas and North Carolina.

Based on this information, Roosevelt publicly announced his support for repeal. This clinched the Democratic nomination for him, and his acceptance speech confirmed his stand: "This convention wants repeal. Your candidate wants repeal. And I am confident that the United States of America wants repeal."[96]

The 1932 election was a massive, record-breaking victory for Roosevelt and the Democrats. Roosevelt won 472 electoral votes against just 59 for Hoover. In the same election, voters sent a mainly Democratic, and mainly prorepeal, majority to Congress. Furthermore, in the same elections nine more state legislatures voted to repeal their own local dry laws.

Rolling Toward Repeal

The Democratic victory signaled the end of Prohibition. Following his nomination, Roosevelt had predicted, "From this date on, the Eighteenth Amendment is doomed."[97] He was right.

The new Congress drafted a repeal amendment with remarkable ease and speed. In December 1932, just one month after the election, the resolution to create the Twenty-First Amendment to the Constitution, nullifying the Eighteenth Amendment, passed both houses in just three days. This speed can be attributed to the mood of Congress, which considered repeal crucial to the country's economic well-being. A law that had radically changed American life for more than a decade was about to be quickly discarded. Pegram writes, "Tangled in the wreckage of Hoover's reputation, and taking on the aspect of an unnecessary burden in a time of national emergency, prohibition was jettisoned . . . with unusual speed and few second thoughts."[98]

However, it would be several months before the states would ratify the new amendment; as the Constitution stipulated, a three-fourths majority of states would have to approve the Twenty-First Amendment for it to become law. In the meantime, Roosevelt asked Congress to modify the Volstead Act by cutting funding for enforcement and increasing the alcoholic content of beer and wine. The House and Senate readily agreed to this partial repeal.

The public also responded enthusiastically. Just after midnight on April 7, 1933, the date on which "real" beer became legal again, a specially decorated beer truck from the Abner Drury Brewery in Washington, D.C., pulled up in front of the White House. A sign on the side read, "Here's to you, President Roosevelt. The nation's first real beer in years."[99] Workers carried two cases of beer into the president's home as a crowd that had spontaneously formed near the beer truck sang the 1930 hit "Happy Days Are Here Again."

Repeal Is Approved

While partial repeal came into force, the process for repealing the Eighteenth Amendment completely was moving swiftly ahead. In February 1933, Congress submitted the Twenty-First Amendment to the individual states. It was a mere three sentences long, the same length as the amendment it sought to nullify.

Ratification by the states was nearly as swift as the passage of the amendment through Congress. On December 5, 1933, the secretary of state formally declared that the necessary majority, thirty-six of the forty-eight states, had approved it. (Alaska and Hawaii were not yet states.) Repeal would take place immediately.

The announcement was celebrated across the country. People held drinking parties and organized parades. They also flocked to newly reopened taverns, which quickly ran out of their supplies of liquor. It has been estimated that almost a million and a half barrels of legal beer were consumed within the first twenty-four hours of repeal.

Celebrities also joyously observed the return of legal alcohol. In Hollywood, actress Jean Harlow smashed a beer bottle on a truckload of 3.2 percent "real" beer bound for restaurants and hotels. And in New York, comedian Jimmy Durante—known as "the Old Schnozzola"

because of his large nose—sang, "Roses are red, violets are blue / I'll
dunk my nose in three point two."[100]

The Lessons of Prohibition

The end of Prohibition did not end the nation's economic troubles, as
many had hoped. The Great Depression lasted for several more years,
until America entered World War II in 1941 and defense spending
boosted the economy.

However, Prohibition did leave a lasting legacy—both positive and
negative—in social history and public policy. Its lessons are still valu-
able, since the issues raised by Prohibition have direct parallels to
many of today's difficult issues.

Perhaps Prohibition's most important lesson concerns laws that
can be reasonably enforced. A law is useful to a democratic society
only if it can be enforced in a reasonable way—that is, without re-
sorting to excessive force or expense. As America discovered, it was
virtually impossible to reasonably enforce a ban on alcohol in a country as vast as the United States. Complete enforcement would have
meant creating a virtual police state, and would have required enormous amounts of money and manpower. The results would not have
been worth the costs.

A Changed Place

Thomas R. Pegram, in his book Battling Demon Rum: The Struggle for a Dry America, summarizes some positive aspects of the Prohibition Era.

"The nightclubs, cafes, bars, and restaurants in which Americans drank after prohibition were not simply saloons with new names but elements of a new culture of entertainment which differed from the saloon-centered nineteenth-century world of drinking. More immediately, prohibition curtailed, at least temporarily, the working-class drinking that had worried progressive observers at the turn of the century. Illegal liquor, though available in cities, was too expensive for most working-class incomes.

Some evidence indicates that the context of drinking and the behavior it produced also changed under prohibition. A coal company president told congressional investigators that 'there is some moonshine liquor, some home-brew, and some bootleg, but the old days of the pay-day whoopee are gone. What drinking there is, is under cover; the practice of drinking up a whole month's pay and challenging the world to mortal combat has passed.' In other words, some of the alarming public manifestations of the culture of male drinking had faded."

Unpopular Laws

Another lesson concerns a law's popularity. Prohibition supporters had naïvely assumed that enforcement would be easy because most citizens dutifully obeyed laws, even those they did not like. They further assumed that even those who disapproved of Prohibition would, in time, come to understand its value. Henry Ford, a prominent dry, once remarked, "We must educate the people, and after a time, just as in other social problems, when the truth is known the liquor law will be enforced."[101]

To Prohibition supporters, these assumptions seemed reasonable. Throughout history, most laws have concerned the regulation of behavior, and most people in society have been willing to uphold them to maintain a level of order. However, in the case of Prohibition these assumptions proved untrue. Prohibition was unpopular with too many people who felt that the government had no right to tell them what they could or could not do in their private lives, as long as their actions did not harm others. In the face of a total ban that they considered unreasonable, many were willing to break the law, even if it meant conspiring with criminal gangs. The lesson learned was that it was not enough to simply make a law and expect people to fall in line. As Edward Behr comments, Prohibition proved that "legislation alone is no answer to America's problems."[102]

The Prohibition of Drugs

Prohibition and its shortcomings have clear parallels to some of America's current drug policies. Many social policy experts, citing the lessons of Prohibition, argue that a complete ban on drugs such as heroin, crack cocaine, and marijuana can never be completely effective. They argue that a complete ban creates too many negative consequences, as it did during the 1920s. Crime rates rise, they contend, because rival gangs fight each other and consumers turn to theft to finance their drug purchases. Disease rates also rise, since infection is easily spread through shared needles. Furthermore, crime organizations profit while governments suffer; countless gangs have become rich through drugs, while billions in tax dollars are spent on enforcement. Crime and health issues will dwindle, these advocates assert, if the present ban is replaced with a closely controlled system of legalized production and distribution.

However, politicians have resisted this alternative. They point to one clear difference between the 1920s and today as justification: Alcohol had already been widely accepted before it was banned, and

Vehicles are x-rayed at the U.S.-Mexico border in San Diego to detect drug smuggling. Some people have drawn parallels between current drug policies and Prohibition.

during Prohibition many otherwise law-abiding citizens continued to drink while police looked the other way. In contrast, drugs such as marijuana and heroin have always been used by a minority of people and have no history of public acceptance.

Furthermore, lawmakers worry about problems that might arise from the legalization of drugs. Some are health related, such as increased numbers of addicts and a rise in infectious disease from shared needles. Another is crime: Lawmakers today realize that lifting the prohibition on alcohol did not end organized crime, and worry that legalizing drugs now likewise will do little to curb criminal activity.

Positive Aspects of Prohibition

Although most historians concede that Prohibition was a failure, it did have some positive effects. For example, it created a small step forward in male-female equality by eradicating the culture of the old-fashioned, men-only saloon. During the 1920s it became acceptable for women to drink in speakeasies, just as they enjoyed other new freedoms such as the vote. Bars have generally been open to both sexes ever since. Newsman Elmer Davis wryly notes: "The old days when father spent his evenings at Cassidy's bar with the rest of the boys are gone, and probably gone forever. Cassidy may still be in business . . . and father may still go down there of evenings, but since Prohibition mother goes down with him."[103]

Another positive aspect of Prohibition was its apparent effect on America's consumption of liquor. In 1925 Woodrow Wilson announced, "Prohibition has saved a million lives."[104] The reality may not have been quite that striking, but it was significant nonetheless. The average amount of drinking fell sharply in the years following Prohibition, and for the next half-century remained lower than it had ever been.

In 1971, the U.S. Department of Health, Education, and Welfare released statistics analyzing drinking habits by decade. The average annual figure per person in 1906–1910 was 2.60 gallons; in 1934, it dropped to 0.97; and in 1940 it rose, but only to 1.56. (Records were not kept during Prohibition.) The average continued to remain well below the high mark for almost forty years after repeal. Not until 1970, when consumption rose again, did Americans drink as much as they had at any time before Prohibition.

These statistics seem to show that Prohibition may not have stopped Americans from drinking, but that it did contribute to a decrease in drinking that lasted for several decades. Norman H. Clark notes, "It would be difficult to overemphasize the significance of this change: Americans after Prohibition were drinking less than at any

Women celebrate repeal. Prohibition helped lessen gender inequality by replacing men-only saloons with the speakeasy open to both sexes.

time since they had learned the technology of distillation, and the marked change had surely taken place during the 1920s."[105]

That fact, some observers argue, points to the relative effectiveness of Prohibition. They contend that the Eighteenth Amendment and the Volstead Act may not have been perfect documents, and that Prohibition was not a complete success; nonetheless, it slowed American liquor consumption and broke the nation of its long-standing drinking habit. This issue—the relative merits of Prohibition and similar laws—is still a vital one in this country, and will no doubt continue to spark debate and controversy in the years to come.

Appendix

Excerpts from Original Documents Pertaining to Prohibition.

Document 1: The Eighteenth Amendment

This is the final version of the Eighteenth Amendment. It went into effect on January 17, 1920.

SEC. 1. After one year from the ratification of this article, the manufacture, sale, or transportation of intoxicating liquors within, the importation thereof into, or the exportation thereof from the United States and all territory subject to the jurisdiction thereof for beverage purposes is hereby prohibited.

SEC. 2. The Congress and the several States shall have concurrent power to enforce this article by appropriate legislation.

SEC. 3. This article shall be inoperative unless it shall have been ratified as an amendment to the Constitution by the legislatures of the several States, as provided in the Constitution, within seven years from the date of the submission hereof to the States by the Congress.

Document 2: The Volstead Act, Title II

The National Prohibition Act, better known as the Volstead Act, was a long piece of legislation. The following excerpts include some of the laws and restrictions contained in the act's important Title II.

SEC. 3. No person shall on or after the date when the eighteenth amendment to the Constitution of the United States goes into effect, manufacture, sell, barter, transport import, export, deliver, furnish or possess any intoxicating liquor except as authorized in this Act, and all the provisions of this Act shall be liberally construed to the end that the use of intoxicating liquor as a beverage may be prevented. Liquor for non beverage purposes and wine for sacramental purposes may be manufactured, purchased, sold, bartered, transported, imported, exported, delivered, furnished and possessed, but only as herein provided. . . .

SEC. 6. No one shall manufacture, sell, purchase, transport, or prescribe any liquor without first obtaining a permit from the commissioner to do so, except that a person may, without a permit, purchase and use liquor for medicinal purposes when prescribed by a physician as herein provided, and except that any person who in the opinion of the commissioner is conducting a bona fide hospital or sanitarium engaged in the treatment of persons suffering from alcoholism, may, under such rules, regulations, and conditions as the commissioner shall prescribe, purchase and use, in accordance with the methods in use in such institution, liquor, to be administered to the patients of such institution under the direction of a duly qualified physician employed by such institution. All permits to manufacture, prescribe, sell, or transport liquor, may be issued for one year, and shall expire on the 31st day of December next succeeding the issuance thereof. . . .Permits to purchase liquor shall specify the quantity and kind to be purchased and the purpose for which it is to be used. No permit shall be issued to any person who within one year prior to the application or issuance thereof shall have violated the terms of any permit issued under this Title or any law of the United States or of any State regulating traffic in liquor. No permit shall be issued to anyone to sell liquor at retail, unless the sale is to be made through a pharmacist designated in the permit and duly licensed under the laws of his State. . . .No one shall be given a permit to prescribe liquor unless he is a physician licensed to practice medicine and actively engaged in the practice of such profession. . . . Nothing in this title shall be held to apply to the manufacture, sale, transportation, importation, possession, or distribution of wine for sacramental purposes, or like religious rites, except section 6 . . . and section 10 hereof, and the provisions of this Act prescribing penalties for the violation of either of said sections. No person to whom a permit may be issued to manufacture, transport, import, or sell wines for sacramental purposes or like religious rites shall sell, barter, exchange, or furnish any such to any person not a rabbi, minister of the gospel, priest, or an officer duly authorized for the purpose by any church or congregation, nor to any such except upon an application duly subscribed by him, which application, authenticated as regulations may prescribe, shall be filed and preserved by the seller. The head of any conference or diocese or other ecclesiastical jurisdiction may designate any rabbi, minister, or priest to supervise the manufacture of wine to be used for the purposes and rites in this section mentioned, and the person so designated may, in the discretion of the commissioner, be granted a permit to supervise such manufacture.

SEC. 7. No one but a physician holding a permit to prescribe liquor shall issue any prescription for liquor. And no physician shall prescribe liquor except after careful physical examination of the person for whose use such prescription is sought, or if such examination is found impractical, then upon the best information obtainable, he in good faith believes that the use of such liquor as a medicine by such person is necessary and will afford relief to him from some known ailment. Not more than a pint of spiritous liquor to be taken internally shall be prescribed for use by the same person within any period of ten days and no prescription shall be filled more than once. Any pharmacist filling a prescription shall at the time endorse upon it over his own signature the word "canceled," together with the date when the liquor was delivered, and then make the same a part of the record that he is required to keep as herein provided. . . .

SEC. 18. It shall be unlawful to advertise, manufacture, sell, or possess for sale any utensil, contrivance, machine, preparation, compound, tablet, substance, formula direction, recipe advertised, designed, or intended for use in the unlawful manufacture of intoxicating liquor. . . .

SEC. 21. Any room, house, building, boat, vehicle, structure, or place where intoxicating liquor is manufactured, sold, kept, or bartered in violation of this title, and all intoxicating liquor and property kept and used in maintaining the same, is hereby declared to be a common nuisance, and any person who maintains such a common nuisance shall be guilty of a misdemeanor and upon conviction thereof shall be fined not more than $1,000 or be imprisoned for not more than one year, or both. . . .

SEC. 25. It shall be unlawful to have or possess any liquor or property designed for the manufacture of liquor intended for use in violating this title or which has been so used, and no property rights shall exist in any such liquor or property. . . . No search warrant shall be issued to search any private dwelling occupied as such unless it is being used for the unlawful sale of intoxicating liquor, or unless it is in part used for some business purposes such as a store, shop, saloon, restaurant, hotel, or boarding house. . . .

SEC. 29. Any person who manufactures or sells liquor in violation of this title shall for a first offense be fined not more than $1,000, or imprisoned not exceeding six months, and for a second or subsequent offense shall be fined not less than $200 nor more than $2,000 and be imprisoned not less than one month nor more than five years. Any person violating the provisions of any permit, or who makes any false record, report, or affidavit required by this title, or violates any of the provisions of this title, for which offense a special penalty is not prescribed, shall be fined for a first offense not more than $500; for a second offense not less than $100 nor more than $1,000, or be imprisoned not more than ninety days; for any subsequent offense he shall be fined not less than $500 and be imprisoned not less than three months nor more than two years. . . .

SEC. 30. After February 1, 1920, the possession of liquors by any person not legally permitted under this title to possess liquor shall be prima facie evidence that such liquor is kept for the purpose of being sold, bartered, exchanged, given away, furnished, or otherwise disposed of in violation of the Provisions of this title. . . . But it shall not be unlawful to possess liquors in one's private dwelling while the same is occupied and used by him as his dwelling only and such liquor need not be reported, provided such liquors are for use only for the personal consumption of the owner thereof and his family residing in such dwelling and of his bona fide guests when entertained by him therein; and the burden of proof shall be upon the possessor in any action concerning the same to prove that such liquor was lawfully acquired, possessed, and used. . . .

Notes

Introduction: The Great Experiment

1. Quoted in Paul Fargis and Sheree Bykofsky, eds., *The New York Public Library Desk Reference*. New York: Simon & Schuster, 1989, p. 714.
2. Quoted in Edward Behr, *Prohibition: Thirteen Years That Changed America*. New York: Arcade, 1996, p. 3.
3. Quoted in Norman H. Clark, *Deliver Us from Evil: An Interpretation of American Prohibition*. New York: Norton, 1976, pp. 144–45.
4. Clark, *Deliver Us from Evil*, p. 134.

Chapter 1: Dry Versus Wet: The Years Just Before Prohibition

5. Quoted in Roger A. Bruns, *Preacher: Billy Sunday and Big-Time American Evangelism*. New York: Norton, 1992, p. 154.
6. Herbert Asbury, *The Great Illusion: An Informal History of Prohibition*. New York: Doubleday, 1950, p. 114.
7. Quoted in Thomas R. Pegram, *Battling Demon Rum: The Struggle for a Dry America, 1800–1933*. Chicago: Ivan R. Dee, 1998, p. 97.
8. Larry Engelmann, *Intemperance: The Lost War Against Liquor*. New York: Free Press, 1979, p. 12.
9. Frederick Lewis Allen, *Only Yesterday: An Informal History of the 1920's*. New York: Wiley & Sons, 1997, p. 189.
10. Pegram, *Battling Demon Rum*, p. 107.
11. Quoted in Jack S. Blocker, *American Temperance Movements: Cycles of Reform*. Boston: Twayne, 1989, p. 104.
12. Quoted in William G. McLoughlin Jr., *Billy Sunday Was His Real Name*. Chicago: University of Chicago Press, 1955, p. xx.
13. Quoted in Pegram, *Battling Demon Rum*, p. 113.
14. Clark, *Deliver Us from Evil*, p. 93.
15. Quoted in Pegram, *Battling Demon Rum*, p. 115.
16. Quoted in Pegram, *Battling Demon Rum*, p. 122.
17. Clark, *Deliver Us from Evil*, p. 119.
18. Quoted in Behr, *Prohibition*, p. 59.
19. Pegram, *Battling Demon Rum*, p. 140.
20. Quoted in Pegram, *Battling Demon Rum*, p. 140.
21. Clark, *Deliver Us from Evil*, p. 122.
22. Quoted in Clark, *Deliver Us from Evil*, p. 128.
23. Behr, *Prohibition*, p. 67.
24. Quoted in Pegram, *Battling Demon Rum*, p. 147.

25. Quoted in Behr, *Prohibition*, p. 73.

Chapter 2: John Barleycorn Is Dead: Prohibition Becomes Law

26. Allen, *Only Yesterday*, p. 185.
27. Quoted in Ethan Mordden, *That Jazz! An Idiosyncratic Social History of the American Twenties*. New York: G.P. Putnam's Sons, 1978, p. 145.
28. Quoted in Fargis and Bykofsky, eds., *The New York Public Library Desk Reference*, p. 714.
29. Clark, *Deliver Us from Evil*, p. 131.
30. Quoted in Pegram, *Battling Demon Rum*, pp. 148–49.
31. Quoted in Allen, *Only Yesterday*, p. 15.
32. Quoted in Allen, *Only Yesterday*, p. 15.
33. Pegram, *Battling Demon Rum*, p. 154.
34. Pegram, *Battling Demon Rum*, p. 150.
35. Quoted in Clark, *Deliver Us from Evil*, p. 114.
36. Clark, *Deliver Us from Evil*, p. 132.
37. Quoted in Behr, *Prohibition*, p. 80.
38. Quoted in Behr, *Prohibition*, p. 81.
39. Quoted in Behr, *Prohibition*, p. 81.
40. Quoted in Henry Lee, *How Dry We Were: Prohibition Revisited*. Englewood Cliffs, NJ: Prentice-Hall, 1963, p. 43.
41. Quoted in Lee, *How Dry We Were*, p. 46.
42. Clark, *Deliver Us from Evil*, p. 141.

Chapter 3: The Roots of Temperance in America

43. Blocker, *American Temperance Movements*, p. 3.
44. Lee, *How Dry We Were*, p. 15.
45. Behr, *Prohibition*, p. 9.
46. Bruns, *Preacher*, p. 156.
47. Quoted in Behr, *Prohibition*, p. 14.
48. Quoted in Blocker, *American Temperance Movements*, p. 7.
49. Quoted in Pegram, *Battling Demon Rum*, pp. 14–15.
50. Quoted in Behr, *Prohibition*, p. 17.
51. Quoted in Bruns, *Preacher*, p. 158.
52. Quoted in Lee, *How Dry We Were*, p. 28.
53. Quoted in Pegram, *Battling Demon Rum*, p. 18.
54. Pegram, *Battling Demon Rum*, pp. xi–xii.
55. Behr, *Prohibition*, p. 32.
56. Quoted in Clark, *Deliver Us from Evil*, p. 70.
57. Clark, *Deliver Us from Evil*, p. 71.

58. Quoted in Pegram, *Battling Demon Rum*, p. 100.
59. Quoted in Asbury, *The Great Illusion*, p. 73.
60. Quoted in Behr, *Prohibition*, p. 39.
61. Behr, *Prohibition*, p. 40.

Chapter 4: Bootleggers and Gangsters: The Effects of Prohibition

62. Behr, *Prohibition*, p. 79.
63. Quoted in Behr, *Prohibition*, p. 84.
64. Quoted in Engelmann, *Intemperance*, p. 33.
65. Allen, *Only Yesterday*, p. 188.
66. Quoted in Clark, *Deliver Us from Evil*, p. 159.
67. Clark, *Deliver Us from Evil*, p. 144.
68. Quoted in Behr, *Prohibition*, p. 88.
69. Quoted in Behr, *Prohibition*, p. 1.
70. Quoted in Behr, *Prohibition*, p. 149.
71. Quoted in Lee, *How Dry We Were*, p. 198.
72. Quoted in Lee, *How Dry We Were*, p. 194.
73. Quoted in Behr, *Prohibition*, p. 140.
74. Behr, *Prohibition*, p. 83.
75. Behr, *Prohibition*, p. 153.
76. Quoted in Engelmann, *Intemperance*, p. 112.
77. Quoted in Behr, *Prohibition*, p. 163.
78. Quoted in Engelmann, *Intemperance*, p. 105.
79. Allen, *Only Yesterday*, p. 188.
80. Pegram, *Battling Demon Rum*, p. 158.
81. Allen, *Only Yesterday*, p. 189.
82. Quoted in Pegram, *Battling Demon Rum*, p. 162.
83. Quoted in Mordden, *That Jazz!*, p. 146.

Chapter 5: Drinking Again: Repeal and the Lessons of Prohibition

84. Quoted in Clark, *Deliver Us from Evil*, p. 145.
85. Quoted in Pegram, *Battling Demon Rum*, p. 166.
86. Quoted in Sean Dennis Cashman, *Prohibition: The Lie of the Land.* New York: Free Press, 1979, p. 229.
87. Quoted in Pegram, *Battling Demon Rum*, p. 179.
88. Allen, *Only Yesterday*, p. 71.
89. Quoted in Behr, *Prohibition*, p. 226.
90. Behr, *Prohibition*, p. 228.
91. Quoted in Allen, *Only Yesterday*, p. 193.
92. Clark, *Deliver Us from Evil*, p. 156.

93. Quoted in Clark, *Deliver Us from Evil,* p. 200.
94. Engelmann, *Intemperance,* p. 199.
95. Pegram, *Battling Demon Rum,* p. 182.
96. Quoted in Clark, *Deliver Us from Evil,* p. 205.
97. Quoted in Engelmann, *Intemperance,* p. 218.
98. Pegram, *Battling Demon Rum,* p. 169.
99. Quoted in "Beer at the White House," Associated Press report, April 7, 1933, http://wire.ap.org.
100. Quoted in Lee, *How Dry We Were,* p. 12.
101. Quoted in Engelmann, *Intemperance,* p. 153.
102. Behr, *Prohibition,* p. 242.
103. Quoted in Lee, *How Dry We Were,* p. 5.
104. Quoted in Behr, *Prohibition,* p. 148.
105. Clark, *Deliver Us from Evil,* p. 146.

For Further Reading

Linda Jacobs Altman, *The Decade That Roared: America During Prohibition.* Brookfield, CT: Twenty-First Century Books/Millbrook Press, 1997. Though it has no photos, this is a good, concise history of the Jazz Age, the period from the beginning of Prohibition up to the Great Depression.

James P. Barry, *The Noble Experiment, 1919–33: The Eighteenth Amendment Prohibits Liquor in America.* New York: Franklin Watts, 1972. Nicely illustrated with vintage cartoons and other graphics, but lacking footnotes.

Daniel Cohen, *Prohibition: America Makes Alcohol Illegal.* Brookfield, CT: Millbrook Press, 1995. A good short history of the years of Prohibition, though it has no footnotes and few primary quotations.

Martin Hintz, *Farewell, John Barleycorn: Prohibition in the United States.* Minneapolis, MN: Lerner, 1996. Graphics and good quotes enliven this well-researched book.

Eileen Lucas, *The Eighteenth and Twenty-First Amendments: Alcohol—Prohibition and Repeal.* Springfield, NJ: Enslow, 1998. This is a good introduction.

Works Consulted

Books

Frederick Lewis Allen, *Only Yesterday: An Informal History of the 1920's.* New York: Wiley & Sons, 1997. A classic popular history first published in 1931.

Herbert Asbury, *The Great Illusion: An Informal History of Prohibition.* New York: Doubleday, 1950. An excellent popular history by a well-regarded popular historian.

Edward Behr, *Prohibition: Thirteen Years That Changed America.* New York: Arcade, 1996. A lively popular history of the Prohibition years, by a veteran journalist.

Jack S. Blocker, *American Temperance Movements: Cycles of Reform.* Boston: Twayne, 1989. A scholarly study by a professor of history.

Roger A. Bruns, *Preacher: Billy Sunday and Big-Time American Evangelism.* New York: Norton, 1992. A lively biography of the most famous evangelist of the Prohibition era.

Sean Dennis Cashman, *Prohibition: The Lie of the Land.* New York: Free Press, 1979. This history of the period is well written and informative.

Norman H. Clark, *Deliver Us from Evil: An Interpretation of American Prohibition.* New York: Norton, 1976. Written by a professor of history, this is a classic study of the era of Prohibition.

Larry Engelmann, *Intemperance: The Lost War Against Liquor.* New York: Free Press, 1979. Engelmann, a writer and historian, concentrates on events in Michigan, considered a key state in the alcohol war.

Paul Fargis and Sheree Bykofsky, eds., *The New York Public Library Desk Reference.* New York: Simon & Schuster, 1989. This standard reference guide includes the text of the Eighteenth Amendment.

Henry Lee, *How Dry We Were: Prohibition Revisited.* Englewood Cliffs, NJ: Prentice-Hall, 1963. A lively popular history by a newspaperman who was a cub reporter during Prohibition.

William G. McLoughlin Jr., *Billy Sunday Was His Real Name.* Chicago: University of Chicago Press, 1955. An absorbing biography of the famous antiliquor preacher.

Ethan Mordden, *That Jazz! An Idiosyncratic Social History of the American Twenties.* New York: G.P. Putnam's Son, 1978. This is an eccentric but entertaining book by a writer best known for his work on American popular music.

Thomas R. Pegram, *Battling Demon Rum: The Struggle for a Dry America, 1800–1933.* Chicago: Ivan R. Dee, 1998. This dense, scholarly work by a professor of history focuses on the political efforts of Prohibition advocates.

Periodicals

Gael Fashingbauer Cooper, "Break Out the Bubbly (Tardy Repeal of Prohibition in Minnesota, 1933–34)," *MPLS-St. Paul Magazine,* December 1995.

Internet Sources

"Beer at the White House," Associated Press report, April 7, 1933, http://wire.ap.org.

Websites

History of Alcohol Prohibition (http://mojo.calyx.net). A dryly written but very informative site maintained by the National Commission on Marijuana and Drug Abuse.

The Making of Prohibition (www.brewingtechniques.com). A well-written essay reprinted on a site of interest to craft and home brewers.

Temperance and Prohibition (http://prohibition.history.ohio state.edu). A good overview on a site maintained by the Ohio State University Department of History.

Index

Picture Credits

About the Author

Adam Woog is the author of more than thirty books for adults, young adults, and children. He has a special interest in biography and history. Woog lives with his wife and daughter in his hometown of Seattle, Washington.